T0198693

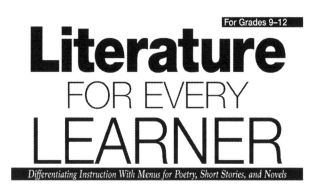

For Grades 9–12

Literature
FOR EVERY
LEARNER

Differentiating Instruction With Menus for Poetry, Short Stories, and Novels

For Grades 9–12

Literature
FOR EVERY
LEARNER

Differentiating Instruction With Menus for Poetry, Short Stories, and Novels

Laurie E. Westphal

Routledge
Taylor & Francis Group

NEW YORK AND LONDON

First published 2014 by Prufrock Press Inc.

Published 2021 by Routledge
605 Third Avenue, New York, NY 10017
2 Park Square, Milton Park, Abingdon, Oxon OX14 4RN

Routledge is an imprint of the Taylor & Francis Group, an informa business

Edited by Lacy Compton

Layout and cover design by Raquel Trevino

ISBN 13: 978-1-61821-141-5 (pbk)

TABLE OF CONTENTS

CHAPTER 1

Choice

C hanging
H ow
O verlooked
I ndividuals
C ommunicate
E xcellence

Choice in the Secondary Classroom

When considering choice in the secondary classroom, we must first picture our classrooms and our curricula, including the wide range of abilities we may find within a single classroom, even one designated as advanced/honors or Advanced Placement (AP). It has become increasing more popular to implement an inclusive, open door, mixed-ability model in these classrooms. Teachers may find that their classes contain special needs students, on-level students, bilingual/ESL students, and gifted students, all wanting to be successful, all with different needs. Cipani (1995) summarized this situation best in his assessment of the variety of needs found in these "inclusive" classrooms:

Students who are academically gifted, those who have had abundant experiences, and those who have demonstrated proficiency with lesson content typically tend to perform well when instruction is anchored at the "implicit" end of the instructional continuum. In contrast, low-performing students (i.e., students at risk for school failure, students with learning disabilities, and students with other special needs) and students with limited experience or proficiency with lesson content are most successful when instruction is explicit. Students with average academic performance tend to benefit most from the use of a variety of instructional methods that address individual needs. Instructional decisions for most students, therefore, should be based on assessment of individual needs. (pp. 498–499)

Acknowledging that these varied and often contradictory needs arise within a mixed-ability setting can lead to frustration, especially when trying to design one assignment or task that can fit everyone's needs. There are few if any traditional, teacher-directed lessons that can be implicit, explicit, and based on individual needs all at the same time. There is, however, one *technique* that tries to accomplish this: the implementation of choice.

Choice: The Superman of Techniques?

Can the offering of appropriate choices really be the hero when our classrooms have such diversity of abilities? Can it leap buildings in a single bound and meet the needs of our implicit, explicit, and individual interests? If introduced properly, certainly it can. By considering the use and subsequent benefits of choice, it becomes apparent that by offering choices, teachers really can meet the needs of the range of students in such a diverse classroom setting. Ask adults whether they would prefer to choose what to do or be told what to do, and of course, they are going to say they would prefer to have a choice. Students have these same feelings. Students will make choices based on their needs, which makes everyone involved in the classroom experience a little less stressed and frustrated.

Why Is Choice Important to High School Students?

"I need to start deciding where I want to go and what I want to do. I didn't think there would be so many choices. Everyone is trying to figure it out right now."

—High school junior, when asked if choice is important to students their age

First, we have to consider the needs of students during their high school years. During these years, teenagers are struggling to determine who they are as well as what path they are going to follow when they graduate. They are constantly trying new ideas and new experiences as a continuation of the middle school mentality, or perhaps they are looking forward to graduation with the goal of their choices having a positive impact on their GPA or looking good on a college application. During this maturing process, which may begin for some their freshman year, and others later in their high school career, academics may be either of little importance as a carry-over their middle school years or of utmost importance as they look to the future. Knowing this, instruction and higher level products have to engage the individuals these students are working to become; implementing choice as a way to engage these students has many explicit benefits once it has been developed as the center of high-level thinking.

One benefit of choice is its ability to meet the needs of so many different students and their learning styles. Although choice is appropriate for all ability levels, it is especially well received by advanced and gifted students. The Dunedin College of Education (Keen, 2001) conducted a research study on the preferred learning styles and techniques of 250 gifted students. Students were asked to rank different learning options; of the 13 different options described to the students, only one option did not receive at least one negative response. It was the option of having choices. All students may have different learning styles and preferences, yet choice is the one option that meets all students' needs. Unlike younger students, high school students have been engaged in the learning process long enough that they usually can recognize their own strengths and weaknesses, as well their learning styles. By allowing choice, students are able to choose what best fits their learning styles and educational needs.

> *"I like being able to have different types of things to pick from. How many diabolical [didactical] journals do we really need to do?"*
>
> —High school sophomore, English II

Another benefit of choice is a greater sense of independence for the students, as some of them have not had the opportunity to consider their own learning in the past. High school students are approaching college, which requires a greater independence and self-focus. When implementing choice, students will have the opportunity to design and create products based on their own vision, rather than what their teacher envisions for them. When using choice, there is a possibility for more than one "right" product; everyone can make the task he or she has selected his or her own, no matter his or her level of ability. When students would enter my secondary classroom, they often had been trained by previous teachers to produce exactly what the teacher wanted, not what the students thought would be best. Teaching my students that what they envision could be correct (and incredible) was often a struggle. "Is this what you want?" or "Is this right?" were popular questions as we started the school year. After being offered various choice opportunities and experiencing the success that often accompanies their producing quality products that they envision, the students begin to take the responsibility for their work. Allowing students to have choices in the products they create to show their learning helps create independence at any age, or within any ability level. This level of independence is a skill they will need to have mastered before they start college.

> *"I had never heard of a menu before [the teacher] assigned us one. I liked knowing what I was going to do."*
>
> —High school freshman, Advanced Level English I

Strengthened student focus on the required content is a third benefit. When students have choices in the activities they wish to complete, they are more focused on the learning that leads to their choice product. Students become interested and engaged when they learn information that can help them develop a product they would like to create. This excitement can manifest in thought-provoking questions and discussions during a class rather than just hurrying through instruction so they can get to the homework. Students will pay close attention to instruction and have an immediate application for the knowledge being presented in class. It is always a goal that all of our secondary students will be intrinsically motivated and focused on the materials being presented; the use of choices in the classroom will bring us closer to attaining this goal.

The final benefit (and I am sure there are many more), is the simple fact that by offering varied choices at appropriate levels, implicit instructional options (and their counterpart, explicit instructional options), as well as individual needs, can be addressed without anyone getting overly frustrated or overworked. Many a great educator has referred to the idea that the best learning takes place when the students have a desire to learn and can feel successful during the process. Some secondary students have a desire to be taught information, others prefer to explore and learn things that is new to them, still others do not want to learn anything unless it is of interest to them. By incorporating different activities from which to choose, students can stretch beyond what they already know, and teachers can create a void that needs to be filled in order for students to complete a product they have selected for themselves. This void leads to a desire to learn.

A Point to Ponder: Making Good Choices Is a Skill

"Even if my students know how to make choices already, I can certainly reinforce the process."

—Secondary teacher

When we consider making good choices as a skill, much like writing an effective paragraph, it becomes easy enough to understand the processes needed to encourage students to make their own choices. In keeping with this analogy, students could certainly figure out how to write on their own, perhaps even how to compose sentences and paragraphs by modeling other examples. Imagine, however, the progress and strength of the writing produced when students are given guidance and even the most basic of instruction on how to accomplish the task. Even with instruction from the teacher, the written piece is still their own, but the quality of the finished piece is so much stronger when guidance is provided during the process. The same is true with the quality of choices students can make when it comes to their instruction and showing their level of knowledge in the classroom.

As with writing, students could make their own choices; however, when the teacher provides background knowledge and assistance, the choices become more meaningful and the products a student chooses to create become richer. Certainly all students could benefit from guidance in the choice-making process, but sometimes our on-level and special needs students may need the most help;

they may not have been in an educational setting that has allowed them to experience different products and the idea of choice can be new to them. Some students may only have experienced basic instructional choices like choosing between two journal prompts or perhaps the option of making a poster or a PowerPoint about the content being studied. Other students may not have experienced even this level of choice. This can cause frustration for both teacher and student.

Teaching Choices as a Skill

So what is the best way to provide this guidance and develop the skill of making good choices? First, select the appropriate number of choices for your students. Although the goal may be to have students choose between 12 different options, teachers might start by having their students choose between three predetermined choices the first day (if they were using a meal menu, students might choose a breakfast activity). Then, after those products have been created and submitted for grading, students can choose between another three options a few days later, another three perhaps the following week, and the final three on the last week. By breaking the choices into smaller manageable pieces, teachers are reinforcing how to approach a more complex and/or varied situation that involves choice in the future. All students can work up to making complex choices with longer lists of options as their choice skill-level increases.

Second, although teenagers crave their independence, they may still need guidance on how to select the option that is best for them. They may not automatically gravitate toward varied options without an excited and detailed description of each choice. For the most part, students have been trained to produce what the teacher requests, which means that when given a choice, they will usually try to ferret out what the teacher wants them to produce. That means that when the teacher discusses the different menu options, the teacher will need to be equally as excited about each. The discussion of the different choices has to be animated and specific. For example, if the content is all very similar, the focus would be on the product: "If you want to do some singing, this one is for you!" or "If you want to write and draw, mark this one as a maybe!" Sometimes, choices may differ based on both content and product, in which case, both can be pointed out to students to assist them in making a good choice. "You have some different choices for this novel's menu, if you would like to work with creating new endings as well as drawing, check this one as a maybe. If you are thinking you want to act and work with the characters, this one might be for you!" This thinking aloud or teacher feedback helps the students begin to see how they might approach different choices. The more exposure they have to the processing the teacher provides, the more skillful they become in their choice making.

How Can Teachers Provide Choices?

"The GT students seem to get more involved in assignments when they have choice. They have so many creative ideas and the menus give them the opportunity to use them."

—Secondary teacher

When people go to a restaurant, the common goal is to find something on the menu to satisfy their hunger. Students come into our classrooms having a hunger, as well—a hunger for learning. Choice menus are a way of allowing our students to choose how they would like to satisfy that intellectual hunger. At the very least, a menu is a list of choices that students use to select an activity (or activities) they would like to complete in order to show what they have learned. At best, it is a complex system in which a student earns points toward a goal determined by the teacher or the student. The points are assigned to products based on the different levels of Bloom's revised taxonomy and the choices may come from different areas of study. If possible, a menu should also incorporate a free-choice option for those "picky eaters" who would like to make a special order to satisfy their needs.

The next few sections provide examples of different menu formats that will be used in this book. Each menu has its own benefits, limitations or drawbacks, and time considerations. An explanation of the free-choice option and its management will follow the information on each type of menu.

Meal Menu

"I found the (meal) menu a great alternative for my students who needed modifications. The idea of different meals made it easy for them to understand."

—Secondary teacher, when asked which menu worked well with inclusive students.

Description

The Meal menu (see Figure 1.1) is a menu with a total of at least nine predetermined choices as well as two or more enrichment/optional activities for students. The choices are created at the various levels of Bloom's revised taxonomy (Anderson & Krathwohl, 2001) and incorporate different learning styles, with the levels getting progressively higher and more complex as students progress from breakfast to lunch and then to dinner. All products carry the same weight for grading and have similar expectations for completion time and effort. The enrichment or optional (dessert) options can be used for extra credit or can replace another meal option at the teacher's discretion.

Benefits

Great starter menu. This menu is very straightforward and easy to understand, so time is saved in presenting the completion expectations.

Flexibility. This menu can cover either one topic in depth or three different objectives or aspects within a topic, with each meal representing a different aspect. With this menu, students have the option of completing three products: one from each meal.

Optional enrichment. Although not required, the dessert category of the meal menu allows students to have the option of going further or deeper if time during the unit permits.

Chunkability. The meal menu is very easy to break apart into smaller pieces. Whether you have students who need support in making choices or you only want to focus on one aspect of a story at a time, this menu can accommodate these decisions. Students could be asked to select a breakfast while the rest of the menu is put on hold until the breakfast product is submitted, then a lunch product is selected, and so on.

Friendly design. Students quickly understand how to use this menu because of its real-world application.

Weighting. All products are equally weighted, so recording grades and maintaining paperwork are easily accomplished with this menu.

Short time period. This menu is intended for shorter periods of time, between 1–3 weeks.

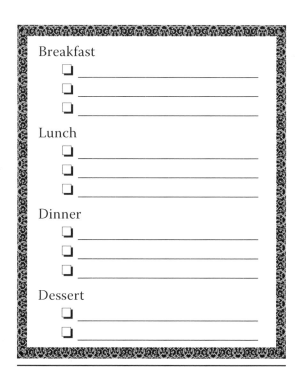

Figure 1.1. Meal menu.

Limitations

None.

Time Considerations

The meal menu is usually intended for shorter amounts of completion time—at the most, it should take 3 weeks with students working outside of class and submitting one product each week. If a menu focuses on one topic in-depth and the students have time in class to work on their products, the menu could be completed in one week.

Poetry Shape Menu

Description

The Poetry Shape menu (see Figure 1.2) is a menu that has been specifically designed for poems. Its format is unique as it allows teachers to determine whether to provide three, six, or nine choices for their students. The number of choices is often determined by the amount of time the teacher plans to spend with the study of the work. The choices are created at the various levels of Bloom's revised taxonomy (Anderson & Krathwohl, 2001) and incorporate different learning styles. All products within the same row carry the same weight for grading and have similar expectations for completion time and effort.

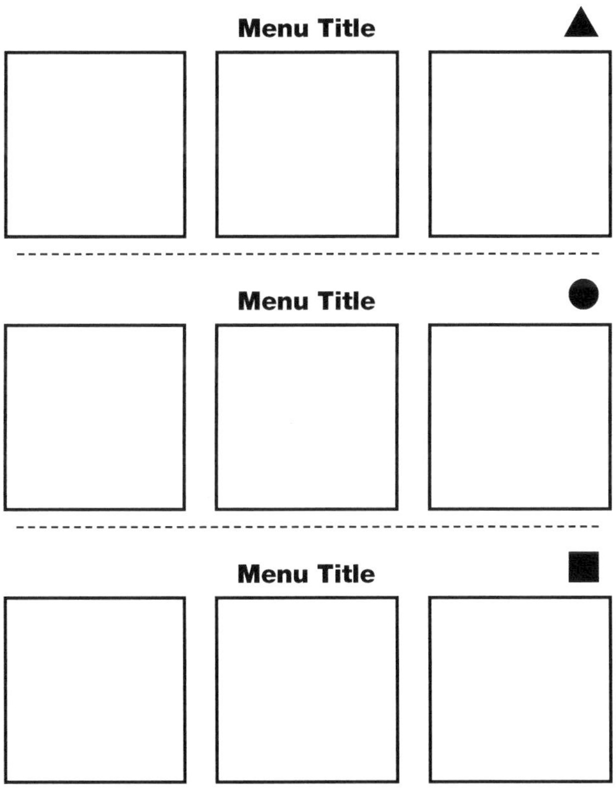

Menu Title ▲

Menu Title ●

Menu Title ■

Figure 1.2. Poetry Shape menu.

Benefits

Flexibility. This menu offers the opportunity for students to create one, two, or three products based on the amount of time spent on the study of the poem. If the teacher only has time for students to create one product, he may give students a strip of choices (triangle, circle, square), which have been tiered based on modifications.

Friendly design. Students quickly understand how to use this menu. It is easy to explain how to make the choices based on the divisions located on the page.

Weighting. All products are equally weighted, so recording grades and maintaining paperwork are easily accomplished with this menu.

Short time period. This menu is intended for a short period of time, at most one week.

Limitations

None.

Time Considerations

This menu is usually intended for a short amount of completion time, based on the amount of time spent on the poem—at the most, it should take one week. If the teacher chooses to provide students with a single tiered ability strip, it could be completed in one or two class periods.

Tic-Tac-Toe Menu

> *"I had the Tic-Tac-Toe before in middle school. I liked it then and still like it now. It has just the right amount of choices on it."*
>
> **—High school freshman, English I, on-level**

Description

The Tic-Tac-Toe menu (see Figure 1.3) is a well-known, commonly used menu that contains a total of eight predetermined choices and, if appropriate, one free choice for students. Choices can be created at the same level of Bloom's revised taxonomy (Anderson & Krathwohl, 2001), or be arranged in such a way as to allow for the three different levels or even three different content areas. If all of the choices have been created at the same level of Bloom's revised taxonomy, each choice carries the same weight for grading and has similar expectations for completion time and effort.

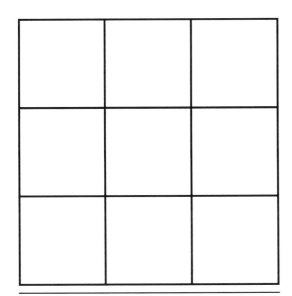

Figure 1.3. Tic-Tac-Toe menu.

Benefits

Flexibility. This menu can cover one topic in depth, or three different topics, objectives, or even content areas. When this menu covers just one objective and all tasks are from the same level of Bloom's revised taxonomy, students have the option of completing three projects in a tic-tac-toe pattern, or simply picking three from the menu. When it covers three objectives or different levels of Bloom's revised taxonomy, students will need to complete a tic-tac-toe pattern (either a vertical column or horizontal row) to be sure they have completed one activity from each objective or level.

Stretching. When students make choices on this menu completing a row or column, based on its design, they will usually face one choice that is out of their comfort zone, be it through its level of Bloom's revised taxonomy, product learning style, or content. They will complete this "uncomfortable" choice because they want to do the other two options in that row or column.

Friendly design. Students quickly understand how to use this menu. It is nonthreatening because it does not contain points, and therefore seems to encourage students to stretch out of their comfort zone.

Weighting. All projects are equally weighted, so recording grades and maintaining paperwork are easily accomplished with this menu.

Short time period. This menu is intended for shorter periods of time, between 1–3 weeks.

Limitations

Few topics. This menu only covers one or three topics.

Student compromise. Although this menu does allow for choice, a student will sometimes have to compromise and complete an activity he or she would not have chosen because it completes the required tic-tac-toe. (This is not always bad, though!)

Time Considerations

This menu is usually intended for shorter amounts of completion time—at the most, this menu should take 3 weeks with one product submitted each week. If a Tic-Tac-Toe menu focuses on one topic in-depth and the students have time in class to work on their products, the menu could be completed in one week.

List Menu

"I like that you can add up the points to be over 100, so even if you make some small mistakes, your grade could still be a 100."

—Secondary student, when asked how he felt about a recent List menu

Description

The List menu (see Figure 1.4), or Challenge List, has a total of at least 10 predetermined choices, each with its own point value, and at least one free choice for students. Choices are simply listed with assigned points based on the levels of Bloom's revised taxonomy (Anderson & Krathwohl, 2001). The choices carry different weights and have different expectations for completion time and effort. A point criterion is set forth that equals 100%, and students choose how they wish to attain that point goal. There are two versions of the List menu included in this book: the Challenge List (one topic in depth) and the Three-Topic List menu (which based on its structure can accommodate multiple topics).

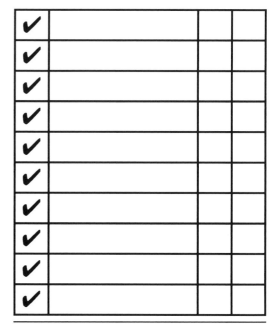

Figure 1.4. List menu.

Benefits

Responsibility. Students have complete control over their grades. They really like the idea that they can guarantee their grades if they complete their required work and meet the expectations set forth in the rubric. If students do not earn full credit on one of the chosen products, they can complete another to be sure they have met their goal. This responsibility over their own grades also allows a shift in thinking about grades—whereas students may think of grades in terms of how the teacher judged their work, or what the teacher gave them, having control over their grades leads students to understand that they earn their grades.

Different learning levels. This menu also has the flexibility to allow for individualized contracts for different learning levels within the classroom. Because there can be many ability levels within a classroom, it may be necessary to contract students based on their ability or even results from the pretesting of content, in which case each student can contract for a certain number of points for his or her 100%.

Concept reinforcement. This menu also allows for an in-depth study of material; however, with the different levels of Bloom's revised taxonomy being represented, students who are still learning the concepts can choose some of the lower level point value products to reinforce the basics before jumping into the higher-level activities.

Variety. A list menu offers a larger variety of product choices. There is guaranteed to be a product of interest to everyone. (And if there isn't, there is always free choice!)

Limitations

One topic. This menu is best used for one topic in depth, so that students don't miss any specific content.

Preparation. Teachers need to have all materials ready at the beginning of the unit for students to be able to choose any of the activities on the list, which requires advanced planning.

Time Considerations

The List menu is usually intended for shorter amounts of completion time—at the most, 2 weeks. (*Note*: Once the materials are assembled, the preparation is minimal!)

20-50-80 Menu

"The 20-50-80 was my favorite. I only had to do two choices to get my 100, but if I had messed up, I could have done another one to make up for it. I like that."

—Junior, AP English III

Description

A 20-50-80 menu (see Figure 1.5), has activities that are worth 20, 50, or 80 points. It is a variation on a List menu, with a total of at least eight predetermined choices: at least two choices with a point value of 20, at least four choices with a point value of 50, and at least two choices with a point value of 80. Choices are assigned points based on the levels of Bloom's revised taxonomy (Anderson & Krathwohl, 2001). Choices with a point value of 20 represent the remember and understand levels, choices with a point value of 50 represent the apply and analyze levels, and choices with a point value of 80 represent the evaluate and create levels. All levels of choices carry different weights and have different expectations for completion time and effort. Students are expected to earn 100 points for a 100%. Students choose what combination they would like to use to attain that point goal.

Benefits

Responsibility. With this menu, students have complete control over their grades.

Low stress. This menu is one of the shortest menus and if students choose well, only requires students to complete two products. This menu is usually not as daunting as some of the longer, more complex menus. It provides students a great introduction into the process of making choices.

Guaranteed activity. This menu's design is also set up in such a way that students must complete at least one activity at a higher level of Bloom's revised taxonomy in order to reach their point goal.

Limitations

One topic. This menu works best with in-depth study of one topic.

Higher level thinking. Students usually choose to complete only one activity at a higher level of thinking.

Time Considerations

The 20-50-80 menu is usually intended for a shorter amount of completion time—at the most, one week.

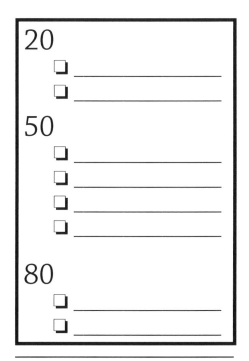

Figure 1.5. 20-50-80 menu.

Free Choice in the Mixed-Ability Classroom

"I don't know if I really liked it at first. It's a lot easier to just do the basic stuff and get it over with but when [the teacher] told us she wanted us to submit at least one free choice, I really got into it! I mean, I could do something I wanted to do? How often do you get to do THAT in school?"

—Secondary GT student

Most of the menus included in this book allow students to submit a free choice as a product. This free choice is a product of their choosing that addresses the content being studied and shows what the student has learned about the topic. Although this option is offered, students may not fully understand its benefits or immediately respond to the opportunity even after it has been explained. Although certain students may have experienced choice before and may be very excited by the idea of taking charge of their own learning, other students, especially those with special needs, may not have had much exposure to this concept. Their educational experiences tend to be objective based and teacher driven. This is not to say that these students would not respond well to the idea of free choice; in fact, they can embrace it as enthusiastically as gifted students. The most significant difference between these two groups successfully approaching free choice is the amount of content needed by the student before he or she embarks on the proposed option. Special needs students need to feel confident in their knowledge of the content and information before they are ready to step out on their own, propose their own idea, and create their unique product.

The menus in this book that include a free choice option require that students submit a free choice proposal form for their teacher's consideration. Figure 1.6 shows two sample proposal forms that have been used many times successfully in my mixed-ability classroom. With certain secondary students, this cuts down greatly on the whining that often accompanies any task given to students. The form used is based on the type of menu being presented. If students are using the Tic-Tac-Toe, Meal, or Poetry Shape menu, there is no need to submit a point proposal form. A copy of these forms should be provided to each student when a menu is first introduced. A discussion should be held with the students so they understand the expectations of a free choice. I always have a few students who do not want to complete a task on the menu; they are welcome to create their own free choice and submit it for approval. The biggest complainers will not always go to the trouble to complete the form and have it approved, but it is

Name: _____   Teacher's Approval: _____

Free-Choice Proposal Form for Point-Based Menu

Points Requested: _____   Points Approved: _____

<u>Proposal Outline</u>

1. What specific topic or idea will you learn about?

2. What criteria should be used to grade it? (Neatness, content, creativity, artistic value, etc.)

3. What will your product look like?

4. What materials will you need from the teacher to create this product?

Name: _____   Teacher's Approval: _____

Free-Choice Proposal Form

<u>Proposal Outline</u>

1. What specific topic or idea will you learn about?

2. What criteria should be used to grade it? (Neatness, content, creativity, artistic value, etc.)

3. What will your product look like?

4. What materials will you need from the teacher to create this product?

Figure 1.6. Sample proposal forms for free choice.

their choice not to do so. The more free choice is used and encouraged, the more students will begin to request it. How the students show their knowledge will begin to shift from teacher-focused to student-designed activities. If students do not want to make a proposal using the proposal form after the teacher has discussed the entire menu and its activities, they can place the unused form in a designated place in the classroom. Other students may want to use their form, and it is often surprising who wants to submit a proposal form after hearing about the opportunity!

Proposal forms must be submitted before students begin working on their free-choice products. The teacher then knows what the student should be working on and the student knows the expectations the teacher has for that product. Once approved, the forms can easily be stapled to the student's menu sheet for reference during the creation and grading process. The student can refer to it as he or she develops his or her free-choice product, and when the grading takes place, the teacher can refer to the proposed agreement for the "graded" features of the product.

Each part of the proposal form is important and needs to be discussed with students:

- *Name/Teacher's Approval.* The student must submit this form to the teacher for approval. The teacher will carefully review all of the information, discuss any suggestions or alterations with the student, if needed, and then sign the top.
- *Points Requested.* Found only on the point-based menu proposal form, this is where negotiation may need to take place. Students usually will submit their first request for a very high number (even the 100% goal). They tend to equate the amount of time a product will take with the amount of points it should earn. Please note, however, that the points are always based on the levels of Bloom's revised taxonomy. For example, a PowerPoint presentation with a vocabulary word quiz would get minimal points, although it may have taken a long time to create. If the students have not been exposed to the levels of Bloom's revised taxonomy, this can be difficult to explain. You can always refer to the popular "Bloom's verbs" to help explain the difference between time requirements and higher level activities.
- *Points Approved.* Found only on the point-based menu proposal form, this is the final decision recorded by the teacher once the point haggling is finished.
- *Proposal Outline.* This is where the student will tell you everything about the product he or she intends to complete. These questions should be completed in such a way that you can really picture what the student is

planning on creating. This also shows you that the student has thought out what he or she wants to create.

o *What specific topic or idea will you learn about?* Students need to be specific here. It is not acceptable to just write "reading" or the title of the novel, story, or poem. This is where they look at the objectives or standards of the unit and choose which one their product demonstrates.

o *What criteria should be used to grade it?* Although there are guidelines for most of the products that the students might create, it is important for the students to explain what criteria are most important to evaluate the product. The student may indicate that the guidelines being used for the predetermined project is fine; however, he or she may also want to add other criteria here.

o *What will your product look like?* It is important that this be as detailed as possible. If a student cannot express what it will "look like," then he or she has probably not given the free-choice plan enough thought.

o *What materials will you need from the teacher to create this product?* This is an important consideration. Sometimes students do not have the means to purchase items for their project. This can be negotiated, as well, but if you ask what students may need, then they often will develop even grander ideas for their free choice.

CHAPTER 2

How to Use Menus in the Classroom

There are different ways to use instructional menus in the classroom. In order to decide how to implement a menu, the following questions should be considered:

- How much prior knowledge of the topic being taught do the students have before the unit or lesson begins?
- How confident are your students in making choices and working independently?
- How much intellectually appropriate information is readily available for students to obtain on their own?

After considering these questions, it becomes easier to determine how menus can be best implemented.

Building Background Knowledge or Accessing Prior Knowledge

"I have students with so many different experiences—sometimes I spend more time than I allotted to review and get everyone up to speed before we get started."

—Social studies teacher

There are many ways to use menus in the classroom. One way that is often overlooked is using menus to access or build background knowledge before a unit begins. This is frequently used when students have had exposure to upcoming content in the past, perhaps during the previous year's instruction, or through similar life experiences. Although they may have been exposed to the content previously, students may not remember the content details at the level needed to proceed with this year's instruction immediately. A shorter menu (the 20-50-80 menu is great for this) covering the previous years' objectives can be provided during the week prior to the new unit so students have the opportunity to recall and engage the information in a meaningful way before they are put on the spot to use it. Students are then ready to take it to a deeper level during this year's unit. For example, a week before starting a unit on *The Book Thief*, the teacher may use a short menu on World War II, knowing that the students may have had the content in the past and should be able to successfully work independently on the menu by engaging their prior knowledge. By offering a menu on the events of the war, students will have a greater understanding of the events in the novel, and very little class time was taken for the prenovel background work. Students can work on products from the menu as anchor activities and homework throughout the week prior to *The Book Thief* unit, with all products being submitted prior to its initiation. The students have been working independently on the topic for at least one week and are ready to begin the novel.

Enrichment and Supplemental Activities

"I have some students who are always finishing early. I hate to just have them read ahead or do more questions since they end up finishing the novel before everyone else, which can cause its own set of frustrations."

—English teacher

Integrating menus into instruction for enrichment and as supplementary activities are the most common uses for menus in the classroom. In this case, the students usually do not have a lot of background knowledge and the intellectually appropriate information about the topic may not be readily available to all students. The teacher will introduce the menu and the activities at the beginning of a unit. The teacher will then progress through the necessary content at the normal rate, using his or her own curricular materials and periodically allowing class time and homework time throughout the unit for students to work on their menu choices to supplement a deeper understanding of the information being presented. This method is very effective, as it builds in an immediate use for the information the teacher is covering. For example, at the beginning of a novel unit on *The Scarlet Letter*, the teacher many introduce the menu with the explanation that students may have not read enough of the novel to complete all of their choices yet. During the unit, however, as they read further, they will be prepared to work on the choices in which they are interested. If students want to work ahead, they certainly can read ahead of the class, but that is not required. Although gifted students often see this as a challenge and will begin to tear through a novel before the teacher discusses each chapter, special needs students begin to develop questions about upcoming events and are ready to ask them when the class gets to that point in the novel. As teachers, we often fight the battle of having students read ahead or "come to class prepared to discuss and question." By introducing a menu at the beginning of a novel and allowing students to complete products as reading progresses, the students naturally begin looking forward and come to class prepared without it being a completely separate requirement.

Mainstream Instructional Activities

> *"I had thought of running simultaneous literature groups but was not sure how to best manage the time in class and keep everyone on task with their novels. I found [that the] menus for each novel kept the groups focused on their novels but also interested in what others were working on. A+."*
>
> —High school English teacher

Another option for using menus and choice in the classroom is to replace certain whole-class curricular activities the teacher uses to teach specific aspects of a novel. In this case, the students may have some limited background knowledge about the literary elements and information is readily available for them in their classroom resources. The teacher would pick and choose which aspects must be directly taught to the students in the large group or small groups, and which could be appropriately learned and reinforced through product menus. The novel unit is then designed using formal instructional large-group lessons, smaller informal group lessons, and specific menu days where the students will use the menu independently to reinforce the prior knowledge they have already learned. In order for this option to be effective, the teacher must feel very comfortable with the students' prior knowledge level, their reading levels, and their readiness to work independently.

Flipped Classroom Activities

> *"Menus make all the difference in the success of my flipped classroom."*
>
> —Secondary teacher

The idea of choice fits hand-in-hand with the philosophy of flipped instruction or the flipped classroom model. When using flipped instruction, the goal is that the students acquire basic information needed through outside sources such as videos, PowerPoint presentations, or other sources their teacher has selected for them. In the case of a novel study, rather than reading the novel aloud round-robin format, students will be responsible for reading sections of the book independently, outside of the classroom. This may mean the students are sitting down at home and reading to themselves, watching a video of the story being read by the author, or listening to an audio recording of the necessary pages. No matter how they have "read" the pages, when the students return to class, their time is spent on quality activities and products based on their reading outside of the classroom. Because the methods students use to read the material are varied, logically, it would work best if the activities within the classroom are varied as well. A menu that outlines all of the activities students can work with during their novel study can be presented at the start of the unit. They can plan their class time and the teacher can support their understanding of their outside reading through discussions and product presentations. Using a menu of options to offer and manage the activities and processing experiences will allow all of the different ability levels within the classroom to feel successful.

Using Leveled Menus With Your Students

"His is different than mine."

—Student in a differentiated classroom

This book contains tiered or leveled menus for each of the included novels, stories, or poems. Although the reading material is the same, each of the three menus may have different values assigned to the same task, slightly different wording for similar tasks, the same product options in a different formatted menu, or even tasks that are only available on certain menus. All of these small modifications make certain menus more appropriate for different students based on their readiness, interest, and ability levels.

As we all know, secondary students tend to compare answers, work, and ideas, and their choices on menus are not any different. Although students may notice the slight differences mentioned above, it may not be an issue when students are working in ability groups, as students are comfortable with having different options based on their grouping. It may also not be an issue when the menus are presented matter-of-factly, stating that everyone is getting a menu that was specifically selected for him or her. Students should rest assured that target numbers (goal of 100 is a 100%) are equal for all of the menus provided and the activities often perceived as the "best" or "most fun" by students are found on all of the versions of the menu. Students should also know that most of the menus have a free choice proposal option so if they really want to do one of the activities found on another menu in the classroom, they are welcome to submit that activity on a free choice proposal form. By presenting tiered menus with confidence and an air for uniquely selecting each menu for its recipient, students are usually willing to proceed with the menu they have received.

> ### *"That's not fair . . ."*
>
> **—Said by at least one student every second in classrooms across the nation**

That being said, you may still have a few students who say, "That's still not fair!" When I first starting using leveled menus with my students, I heard a few comments like this. They quickly dissipated with my standard and practiced responses. Of course, the first response (which they do not always appreciate) is that fair is not equal. I know students do not like to hear this response, as it is hard to argue against this, because it is patently true. Secondly, I remind students that everyone has different strengths and the menus are distributed based on everyone's strengths. Again, they know this; they just do not like to acknowledge it. Lastly, if the students are being especially surly, I sometimes have to play the "parent card," meaning, I am the teacher and I have the right to do what I feel is best for each student. This last option is nonnegotiable and although students may not like it, they understand the tone and sentiment, as they have usually experienced it before at home.

The bottom line when it comes to using tiered menus is that students will respond to the use of seemingly different menus within one classroom based on how the teacher presents or reacts to it. In the past, when I have used different formats, I address the format or obvious differences in a matter-of-fact manner, such as, "I have spiced things up with this menu and have three different ones which I will pass out. You may receive one that is different than your neighbor's but whichever one you receive is going to be lots of fun for you!" Other times, when the menus are very similar in their format and graphics, I just distribute them and address concerns when they are brought up. For the most part, students are more likely to simply go with what they have been given when any differences in menus are presented confidently without being open to debate or complaint.

CHAPTER 3

Guidelines for Products

> *"I appreciate the different choices. I am not much of a puppet person though. I know some people in my class got excited about it."*
>
> —Sophomore, when asked about the different types of products on the latest menu

This chapter outlines the different types of products used in the featured menus, as well as the guidelines and expectations for each. It is very important that students understand the expectations of a completed product before they choose to work on it. By discussing these expectations before students begin and having the information readily available at the time of product selection, you will limit the frustration on everyone's part.

$1 Contract

> *"I really appreciate the $1 form. It kept me from having to run to [craft store] and spend $60 on felt and glitter and all of the other things we normally have to buy for projects."*
>
> —Parent of one of my students when asked for feedback on a recent menu

Consideration should be given to the cost of creating the products included on any menu. The resources available to students vary within a classroom, and students should not be graded on the amount of materials they can purchase to make a product look better. These menus are designed to equalize the resources students have available. The materials for most products are available for less than a dollar and can often be found in a teacher's classroom as part of the classroom supplies. If a product requires materials from the student, a $1 contract is noted as part of the product's guidelines. This is a very important in the explanation of the product. First of all, by limiting the amount of money a student can spend, it creates an equal amount of resources for all. Second, it actually encourages a more creative product; when students are limited by the amount of materials they can readily purchase, they often have to use materials from home in new and unique ways. Figure 3.1 is a sample of the contract that has been used many times in my classroom with various products.

$1 Contract

I did not spend more than $1.00 on my ______________________________.

______________________________ ______________

Student Signature Date

My child, ______________________, did not spend more than $1.00 on the product he or she created.

______________________________ ______________

Parent Signature Date

Figure 3.1. $1 contract.

The Products

Table 3.1 contains a list of the products used in this book. These products were chosen for their flexibility in addressing various learning styles, as well as being popular products most students have experienced; teachers may already be using these in their classroom, which makes the product easy for the students to understand. The products have been sorted by learning style—visual, kinesthetic, or auditory. Each menu has been designed to include products from all of the learning styles. Some of the products may fit into more than one area depending on how they are presented or implemented (and some of the best products crossover between styles), but you will find them listed by their most common application. The specific guidelines for all of the products are presented in an easy-to-read card format that can be reproduced for students. This format is convenient for students to have in front of them when they work on their products.

Product Frustrations

One of the biggest frustrations that accompanies the use of various products on menus is the barrage of questions about the products themselves. Students can become so wrapped up in the products and the criteria for creating them that they do not focus on the content being presented. This is especially true when menus are first introduced to the class. Students can spend an exorbitant amount of time asking the teacher about the products mentioned on the menu. When this happens, what should have been a 10–15 minute menu introduction turns into 45–50 minutes of discussion about product expectations. Most teachers cannot afford to spend even a little time discussing the attributes of a PowerPoint presentation when there is content to be discussed.

Another frustration often comes when showing students product examples. In order to facilitate the introduction of the menu products, teachers may consider showing their students examples of the product(s) from the previous year. Although this can be helpful, it can also lead to additional frustration on the part of both the teacher and the student. Some students may not feel they can produce a product as nice, big, special, or (you fill in the blank) as the example, or when shown an example, take that to mean the teacher would like something exactly like the one they are shown. To avoid this situation, I would propose that, if using examples, the example students are shown be a "blank" example that demonstrates how to create the shell of the product. If an example of a windowpane is needed, for example, then students might be shown a blank piece of paper that is divided into six panes. The students can then take the "skeleton" of the product and make it their own as they create their own version of the windowpane using their information.

Table 3.1
Products

Visual/Written	Kinesthetic	Verbal/Auditory
Acrostic	Board Game	Children's Book
Advertisement	Book Cover	Class Game
Book Cover	Bulletin Board Display	Commercial
Brochure/Pamphlet	Class Game	Game Show
Bulletin Board Display	Collage	Interview
Bumper Sticker	Collection	News Report
Cartoon/Comic Strip	Commercial	Play
Children's Book	Concentration Cards	Power Point—Speaker
Collage	Costume	Presentation of Created
Crossword Puzzle	Cross-Cut Model/Diagram	Product
Diary/Journal	Diorama	Puppet
Drawing	Flipbook	Song/Rap
Essay	Folded Quiz Book	Speech
Folded Quiz Book	Game Show	Student-Taught Lesson
Graphic Novel	Mask	Tell a Story
Greeting Card	Mobile	You Be the Person
Instruction Card	Model	Presentation
Letter	Mural	Video
Map	Museum Exhibit	
Mind Map	Play	
Newspaper Article	Product Cube	
Obituary	Puppet	
Paragraph	Quiz Board	
Picture Dictionary	Scrapbook	
Poster	Student-Taught Lesson	
Power Point—Stand Alone	Three-Dimensional Timeline	
Questionnaire	Trading Cards	
Quiz	Trophy	
Quiz Board	Video	
Recipe	Webquest	
Scrapbook		
Social Media Profile		
Story		
Survey		
Three Facts and a Fib		
Trading Cards		
Venn Diagram		
Window Pane		
Worksheet		

Product Guidelines

"Wow. You know how great these are . . . how much time they will save?"

—A group of teachers, when presented with a page
of products guidelines for their classroom

Most frustrations associated with products can be addressed proactively through the use of standardized, predetermined product guidelines that are shared with students prior to their selecting and subsequently creating any products. These product guidelines are designed in a specific yet generic way, such that anytime throughout the school year that the students select a product, its guidelines will apply. A beneficial side effect of using set guidelines for a product is the security it creates. Students are often reticent to try something new, as it requires taking a risk on their part. Traditionally, when students select products, they ask questions about creating it; hope they remember and understood all of the details and turn it in. It can be quite a surprise when they receive the product back and realize that it was not complete, or did not meet the teacher's expectations. As you can imagine, students may not want to take the risk on something new the next time; they would prefer to do what they know and be successful. Through the use of product guidelines, students can begin to feel secure in their choice of product before they start working on the product itself. If they are not feeling secure, they tend to stay within their comfort zone.

The product guidelines for all of the menu products, as well as some potential free-choice options, are included in an easy-to-read card format (see Figure 3.2). (The guidelines for some products, such as summaries, are omitted because teachers often have different criteria for these products.) Once the products and/or menus have been selected, there are many options available to share this information.

Sharing Product Guidelines With Students

There really is no one "right way" to share the product guideline information with your students. It all depends on their abilities and needs. Some teachers choose to duplicate and distribute all of the product guideline pages to students at the beginning of the year so each student has his own copy in front of him while he works on his products. As another option, a few classroom sets can be created by gluing each product guideline onto separate index cards, hole punching the corner of each card, and placing them on a metal ring. These ring sets can be placed in a central location where students can borrow and return them as they work on their products. Using a ring also allows for the addition of new products as they are introduced to the whole class or through future menus. Some teachers prefer to introduce product guidelines as students experience them on their menus. In this case, product guidelines from the menu currently assigned can be enlarged, laminated, and posted on a bulletin board for easy access during classroom work time. Some teachers may choose to reproduce each menu's specific product guidelines on the back of the menu. No matter which method a teacher chooses to share the information with the students, he or she will save a lot of time and frustration by having the product guidelines available for student reference (e.g., "Look at your product guidelines, I think that will answer your question.")

Story Map

A commonly used analysis tool in an English classroom is the story/novel map. The story map is a quick and effective way for a student to dissect a story and show that he or she can analyze the important parts of the story. Story maps are an option for some of the menus provided in this book. Two examples are offered (see Figures 3.3, 3.4); each coded to match the levels found in the tiered menus. However, teachers who have a favorite format that students are accustomed to should feel free to use their own.

Acrostic	Advertisement	Board Game
• Must be at least 8.5" by 11" • Neatly written or typed • Target word written down the left side of the paper • Each descriptive phrase chosen must begin with one of the letters from the target word • Each descriptive phrase chosen must be related to the target word	• Must be at least 8.5" by 11" • A slogan should be included • Color picture of item or service should be included • Include price, if appropriate • Can be created on the computer	• At least four thematic game pieces • At least 20 colored/thematic squares • At least 15 question/activity cards • Include a thematic title on the board • Include a complete set of rules for playing the game • At least the size of an open file folder
Book Cover	**Brochure/Pamphlet**	**Bulletin Board Display**
• Front cover—title, author, image • Front inside flap—paragraph summary of the book • Back inside flap—brief biography of author with at least three details • Back cover—your comments about the book • Spine—title and author	• Must be at least 8.5" by 11" • Must be in three-fold format; front fold has the title and picture • Must have both pictures and written text • Information should be in paragraph form with at least five facts included • Can be created on computer	• Must fit within assigned space on bulletin board or wall • Must include at least five details • Must have a title • Must have at least five different elements (e.g., posters, papers, questions) • Must have at least one interactive element that engages the reader
Cartoon/Comic Strip	**Children's Book**	**Class Game**
• Must be at least 8.5" by 11" • Must have at least six cells • Must have meaningful dialogue • Must include color	• Must have a cover with book's title and student's name as author • Must have at least 10 pages • Each page should have an illustration to accompany the story • Neatly written or typed • Can be created on the computer	• Game should allow all class members to participate • Must have only a few, easy-to-understand rules • Can be a new variation on a current game • Must have multiple questions • Must provide answer key before game is played • Must be approved by teacher before being played

Figure 3.2. Product guidelines.

Collage	Collection	Commercial/Infomercial
• Must be at least 8.5" by 11" • Pictures must be cut neatly from magazines or newspapers (no clip art from the computer or the Internet) • Label items as required in task	• Has the number of items indicated • All of the items fit within the predetermined space • All items are provided in a box or bag • Do not bring anything valuable as part of your collection	• Must be 1–2 minutes in length • Script must be turned in before the commercial is presented • Can be presented live to an audience or recorded • Should have props or some form of costume(s) • Can include more than one person
Concentration Cards	**Cross-Cut Diagram/Model**	**Crossword Puzzle**
• At least 20 index cards (10 matching sets) must be made • Both pictures and words can be used • Information should be placed on just one side of each card • Include an answer key that shows the matches • All cards must be submitted in a carrying bag	• Must include a scale to show the relationship between the diagram/model and the actual item • Must include details for each layer • If creating a diagram, must also meet the guidelines for a poster • If creating a model, must also meet the guidelines for a model	• At least 20 significant words or phrases should be included • Develop appropriate clues • Include puzzle and answer key • Can be created on the computer
Diary/Journal	**Diorama**	**Drawing**
• Neatly written or typed • Should include the appropriate number of entries • Should include a date if appropriate • Should be written in first person	• Must be at least 4" by 5" by 8" • Must be self-standing • All interior space must be covered with relevant pictures and information • Name written on the back • Informational/title card attached to diorama • $1 contract signed	• Must be at least 8.5" by 11" • Must show what is requested in the task statement • Must include color • Must be neatly drawn by hand • Must have title • Name written on the back

Figure 3.2. Continued.

Essay	Flipbook	Folded Quiz Book
• Neatly written or typed • Must cover the specific topic in detail • Must be at least three paragraphs • Must include resources or bibliography if appropriate	• Must be at least 8.5" by 11" folded in half • All information or opinions are supported by facts • Created with the correct number of flaps cut into the top • Color is optional • Name written on the back	• Must be at least 8.5" by 11" folded in half • Must have at least 10 questions • Created with the correct number of flaps cut into the top • Questions written or typed neatly on upper flaps • Answers written or typed neatly inside each flap • Color is optional • Name written on the back
Game Show	**Graphic Novel**	**Greeting Card**
• Needs an emcee or host • Must have at least two contestants • Must have at least one regular round and a bonus round • Questions will be content specific • Props can be used, but are not mandatory	• Must be bound as a book would be bound • Pages must contain colorful cells • Should contain dialogue • Can be hand drawn or produced on the computer	• Front—colored pictures, words optional • Front inside—personal note related to topic • Back inside—greeting or saying; must meet product criteria • Back outside—logo, publisher, and price for card
Instruction Card	**Interview**	**Letter**
• Must be no larger than 5" by 8" • Created on heavy paper or index card • Neatly written or typed • Uses color drawings • Provides instructions stated in the task	• Must have at least eight questions about the topic being studied • Person chosen for interview must be an "expert" and qualified to provide answers • Questions and answers must be neatly written or typed	• Neatly written or typed • Uses proper letter format • At least three paragraphs in length • Must follow type of letter stated in the menu (e.g., friendly, persuasive, informational)

Figure 3.2. Continued.

Map	Mind Map	Mobile
• Must be at least 8.5" by 11" • Accurate information is included • Includes at least 10 relevant locations • Includes compass rose, legend, scale, and key	• Must be at least 8.5" by 11" • Uses unlined paper • Must have one central idea • Follows the "no more than four" rule—no more than four words coming from any one word • Should be neatly written or developed using a computer	• Includes at least 10 pieces of related information • Includes color and pictures • At least three layers of hanging information • Hangs in a balanced way

Model	Mural	Museum Exhibit
• Must be at least 8" by 8" by 12" • Parts of model must be labeled • Should be in scale if possible • Must include a title card • Name should be permanently written on the model • $1 contract signed	• Must be at least 22" by 54" • Must contain at least five pieces of important information • Must have colored pictures • Words are optional, but a title should be included • Name should be permanently written on the back	• Should have title for exhibit • Must include at least five "artifacts" • Each artifact must be labeled with a neatly written card • Exhibit must fit within the size assigned • $1 contract signed • No expensive or irreplaceable objects in the display

News Report	Newspaper Article	Obituary
• Must address the who, what, where, when, why, and how of the topic • Script of report must be turned in with project (or before if performance will be live) • Must be either performed live or recorded	• Must be informational in nature • Must follow standard newspaper format • Must include picture with caption that supports article • At least three paragraphs in length • Neatly written or typed	• Has a picture of the person (can be hand drawn) • Shares the date (if available), age, and cause of death • Lists the deceased's survivors • Includes information on the person's life and personality

Figure 3.2. Continued.

Paragraph	Picture Dictionary	Play/Skit
• Neatly written or typed • Must have topic sentence, at least three supporting sentences or details, and a concluding sentence • Must use appropriate vocabulary and follow grammar rules	• Must be written neatly or made on the computer • Includes a clear, meaningful picture for each word • Definition written in your own words	• Must be 4–6 minutes in length • Script must be turned in before play is presented • May be presented to an audience or recorded for future showing • Should have props or some form of costume(s) • Can include more than one person
Poster	**PowerPoint—Speaker**	**PowerPoint—Stand Alone**
• Should be the size of a standard poster board • Includes at least five pieces of important information • Must have title • Must contain both words and pictures • Name written on the back • Bibliography included as needed	• At least 10 informational slides and one title slide with student's name • No more than two words per page • Slides must have color and no more than one graphic per page • Animations are optional but should not distract from information being presented • Presentation should be timed and flow with the speech being given	• At least 10 informational slides and one title slide with student's name • No more than 10 words per page • Slides must have color and no more than one graphic per page • Animations are optional but should not distract from information being presented
Product Cube	**Puppet**	**Questionnaire**
• All six sides of the cube must be filled with information • Neatly written or typed • Name must be printed neatly on the bottom of one of the sides • Should be submitted flat for grading	• Puppet should be handmade and must have a moveable mouth • A list of supplies used to make the puppet must be turned in with the puppet • $1 contract signed • If used in a puppet show, must also meet the criteria for a play	• Neatly written or typed • Include at least 10 questions with possible answers, and at least one answer that requires a written response • Questions must be helpful to gathering information on the topic being studied

Figure 3.2. Continued.

Quiz	Quiz Board	Recipe/Recipe Card
• Must be at least a half sheet of paper long • Neatly written or typed • Must cover the specific topic in detail • Must include at least five questions including a short answer question • Must have at least one graphic • An answer key must be turned in with the quiz	• Must have at least five questions • Must have at least five answers • Should use a system with lights • Should be no larger than a poster board • Holiday lights can be used • $1 contract signed	• Must be written neatly or typed on a piece of paper or an index card • Must have a list of ingredients with measurement for each • Must have numbered steps that explain how to make the recipe
Scrapbook	**Social Media Profile**	**Song/Rap**
• Cover of scrapbook must have a meaningful title and student's name • Must have at least five themed pages • Each page will have at least one meaningful picture • All photos must have captions	• Has a picture • Shares basic information about the person or event • Should have at least five friends based on information available • Should follow the format used by the social media site • Should have at least five comments or interactions on the page	• Words must make sense • Can be presented to an audience or taped • Written words must be turned in before performance or with taped song • Should be at least 2 minutes in length
Speech	**Story**	**Survey**
• Must be at least 2 minutes in length • Should not be read from written paper • Note cards can be used • Written speech must be turned in before speech is presented • Voice must be clear, loud, and easy to understand	• Must have all of the elements of a well-written story (setting, characters, conflict, rising action, and resolution) • Must be appropriate length to allow for story elements • Neatly written or typed	• Must have at least five questions related to the topic • Must include at least one adult respondent who is not your teacher • The respondent must sign the survey • Information gathered and conclusions drawn from the survey should be written or presented graphically

Figure 3.2. Continued.

Tell a Story	Three-Dimensional Timeline	Three Facts and a Fib
• Must have all of the elements of a well-written story • Must be long enough to develop the plot and characters • Can be told to teacher or prerecorded	• Must be no bigger than standard-size poster board • Must be divided into equal time units • Must contain at least 10 important dates and have at least two sentences explaining why each date is important • Must have a meaningful object securely attached beside each date to represent that date • Must be able to explain how each object represents each date	• Can be written, typed, or created using PowerPoint • Must include exactly four statements: three true statements and one false statement • False statement should not obvious • Brief paragraph should be included that explains why the fib is false
Trading Cards	**Trophy**	**Venn Diagram**
• Include at least 10 cards • Each card must be at least 3" by 5" • Each should have a colored picture • Includes at least three facts on the subject of the card • Cards must have information on both sides • All cards must be submitted in a carrying bag	• Must be at least 6" tall • Must have a base with the name of the person getting the trophy and the name of the award written neatly or typed on it • Top of trophy must be appropriate and represent the award • Name should be written on the bottom of the award • Must be an originally designed trophy (avoid reusing a trophy from home) • $1 contract signed	• Must be at least 8.5" by 11" • Shapes should be thematic and neatly drawn • Must have a title for entire diagram and a title for each section • Must have at least six items in each section of the diagram • Name written on the back
Video	**WebQuest**	**Windowpane**
• Use VHS, DVD, or Flash format or other recording format • Turn in a written plan with project • Students will need to arrange their own way to record the video or allow teacher at least 3 days notice to set up recording • Covers important information about the project • Name written on the video label	• Must quest through at least three high-quality websites • Websites should be linked in the document • Can be submitted in a Word or PowerPoint document • Includes at least three questions for each website • Must address the topic	• Must be at least 8.5" by 11" unlined paper • Must include at least six squares • Each square must include both a picture and words that should be neatly written or typed • All pictures should be both creative and meaningful • Name should be written on the bottom right-hand corner of the front of the windowpane

Figure 3.2. Continued.

Worksheet	You Be the Person Presentation
• Must be 8.5" by 11" • Neatly written or typed • Must cover the specific topic or question in detail • Must have at least one graphic • An answer key will be turned in with the worksheet	• Take on the role of the person • Cover at least five important facts about the life of the person • Must be 3–5 minutes in length • Script must be turned in before information is presented • Should be presented to an audience with the ability to answer questions while in character • Must have props or some form of costume

Figure 3.2. Continued.

Story Map

▲ ●

Title and Author

Setting

Main Characters

For each main character, write at least three traits and a quote
from the story to support your chosen traits.

Supporting Characters

Write one sentence about why each supporting character is important to the story.

Problem

Figure 3.3. Story map 1.

Story Map

▲ ●

Major Events in the Story

Resolution

Figure 3.3. Continued.

Story Map

Title and Author

Setting
Include at least two quotes that show the setting of the story.

Characters
Write at least three traits for each and a quote from
the story to support your chosen traits

Theme
Select at least one quote that shows theme.

Mood
Select at least one quote that shows mood.

Figure 3.4. Story map 2.

Story Map

Plot

Conflict

Resolution

Figure 3.4. Continued.

CHAPTER 4

Rubrics

"I frequently end up with more papers and products to grade than with a unit taught in the traditional way. Luckily, the rubric speeds up the process."

—Secondary teacher when asked about what
she liked least about using menus

The most common reason teachers feel uncomfortable with menus is the need for equality in grading. Teachers often feel it is easier to grade identical products created by all of the students, rather than grading a large number of different products, none of which looks like any other. The great equalizer for a multitude of different products is a generic rubric that can cover all of the important qualities of an excellent product.

All-Purpose Rubric

Figure 4.1 is an example of a rubric that has been classroom tested with various menus. This rubric can be used with any point value activity presented in a menu, as there are five criteria and the columns represent full points, half points, or no points. Although Tic-Tac-Toe and Meal menus are not point based, this rubric can be used to grade products from these menus. Teachers simply assign 100 points to each of the products students select and then use the all-purpose rubric to grade each product individually based on a total of 100 points.

There are different ways that this rubric can be shared with students. Some teachers prefer to provide it when a menu is presented to students. This rubric can be reproduced on the back of the menu along with its guidelines. The rubric can also be given to students to keep in their folder with their product guideline cards so they always know the expectations as they complete products throughout the school year. Some teachers prefer to keep a master copy for themselves and post an enlarged copy of the rubric on a bulletin board, or provide one copy for parents during open house so they understand how their children's menu products will be graded.

No matter how the rubric is shared with students, the first time they see this rubric, it should be explained in detail, especially the last column titled "Self." It is very important that students self-evaluate their products. This column can provide a unique perspective of the project as it is being graded. *Note*: This rubric was designed to be specific enough that students will know the criteria the teacher is seeking, but general enough that they can still be as creative as they like in the creation of their product.

Student-Taught Lessons and Student Presentation Rubrics

Although the all-purpose rubric can be used for all activities, there are two occasions that seem to warrant a special rubric: student-taught lessons and student presentations. These are unique situations, with many details that must be considered to create a quality product.

Teachers often would like to allow students to teach their fellow classmates, but are concerned about quality lessons and may not be comfortable with the grading aspect of the assignment; rarely do students understand all of the components that go into designing an effective lesson. This student-taught lesson rubric helps focus the student on the important aspects of a well-designed lesson, and allows teachers to make the evaluation process a little more subjective. The student-taught lesson rubric (see Figure 4.2) included for these menus is appropriate for all levels.

Student presentations can be difficult to evaluate. The first consideration with these types of presentations is that of objectivity. The objectivity can be addressed through a very specific presentation rubric that reinforces the expec-

Name: _____

All-Purpose Rubric

Criteria	Excellent (Full Credit)	Good (Half Credit)	Poor (No Credit)	Self
Content Is the content of the product well chosen?	Content chosen represents the best choice for the product. Information or graphics are well chosen and related to content.	Information or graphics are related to content, but are not the best choice for the product.	Information or graphics presented do not appear to be related to the topic or task.	
Completeness Is everything included in the product?	All information needed is included. Product meets the product criteria and the criteria of the task as stated.	Some important information is missing. Product meets the product criteria and the criteria of the task as stated.	Most important information is missing. The product does not meet the task or does not meet the product criteria.	
Creativity Is the product original?	Presentation of information is from a new perspective. Graphics are original. Product includes elements of fun and interest.	Presentation of information is from a new perspective. Graphics are not original. Product has elements of fun and interest.	There is no evidence of new thoughts or perspectives in the product.	
Correctness Is all of the information included correct?	All information presented in the product is correct and accurate.	Not applicable.	Any portion of the information presented in the product is incorrect.	
Communication Is the information in the product well communicated?	All information is neat and easy to read. Product is in appropriate format and shows significant effort. Oral presentations are easy to understand and presented with fluency.	Most of the product is neat and easy to read. Product is in appropriate format and shows significant effort. Oral presentations are easy to understand, with some fluency.	The product is not neat and easy to read or the product is not in the appropriate format. It does not show significant effort. Oral presentation was not fluent or easy to understand.	
			Total Grade:	

Figure 4.1. All-purpose product rubric.

Name: _____

Student-Taught Lesson Grading Rubric

Parts of Lesson	Excellent	Good	Fair	Poor	Self
Prepared and Ready: All materials and lesson ready at start of class period, from warm-up to conclusion of lesson.	**10** Everything is ready to present.	**6** Lesson is present, but small amount of scrambling.	**3** Lesson is present, but major scrambling.	**0** No lesson ready or missing major components.	
Understanding: Presenter understands the material well. Students understand information presented.	**20** All information is correct and in correct format.	**12** Presenter understands; 25% of students do not.	**4** Presenter understands; 50% of students do not.	**0** Presenter is confused.	
Completion: Includes all significant information from section or topic.	**15** Includes all important information.	**10** Includes most important information.	**2** Includes less than 50% of the important information.	**0** Information is not related.	
Practice: Includes some way for students to practice or access the information.	**20** Practice present, well chosen.	**10** Practice present, can be applied effectively.	**5** Practice present, not related or best choice.	**0** No practice or students are confused.	
Interest/Fun: Most of the class is involved, interested, and participating.	**15** Everyone interested and participating.	**10** 75% actively participating.	**5** Less than 50% actively participating.	**0** Everyone off task.	
Creativity: Information presented in imaginative way.	**20** Wow, creative! I never would have thought of that!	**12** Good ideas!	**5** Some good pieces but general instruction.	**0** No creativity; all lecture/ notes/ worksheet.	
				Total Grade:	

Your Topic/Objective:

Comments:

Don't Forget:
All copy requests and material requests must be made at least 24 hours in advance.

Figure 4.2. Student-taught lesson grading rubric.

tations for the speaker. The rubric will need to be discussed and various criteria demonstrated before the students begin preparing their presentations. The second consideration is that of the audience and its interest in the presentation. How frustrating is it to have to grade 30 presentations when the audience is not paying attention, off task, or tuning out? This can be solved by allowing your audience to be directly involved in the presentation by presenting them with a rubric that can be used to provide feedback to their classmates. If all of the students have been instructed on the student presentation rubric (see Figure 4.3) when they receive their feedback rubric, then they will be quite comfortable with the criteria. Students are asked to rank their classmates on a scale of 1–10 in the areas of content, flow, and the prop they chose to enhance their presentation (see Figure 4.4). Students are also asked to state two things the presenter did well. Although most students understand this should be a positive experience for the presenter, it may need to be reinforced that certain types of feedback are not necessary; for example, if the presenter dropped her prop and had to pick it up, the presenter knows this and it probably does not need to be noted again. The feedback should be positive and specific as well. A comment of "Great!" is not what should be recorded; instead, something specific such as, "You spoke loudly and clearly" or "You had great drawings!" should be written on the form. These types of comments really make the students take note and feel great about their presentations. The teacher should not be surprised to note that the students often look through all of their classmates' feedback and comments before ever consulting the rubric the teacher completed. Once students have completed a feedback form for a presenter, the forms can then be gathered at the end of each presentation, stapled together, and given to the presenter at the end of the class.

Name: _____

Student Presentation Rubric

Criteria	Excellent	Good	Fair	Poor	Self
Content Complete Did the presentation include everything it should?	**30** Presentation included all important information about topic being presented.	**20** Presentation covered most of the important information, but one key idea was missing.	**10** Presentation covered some of the important information, but more than one key idea was missing.	**0** Presentation covered information, but the information was trivial or fluff.	
Content Correct Was the information presented accurate?	**30** All information presented was accurate.	**20** All information presented was correct, with a few unintentional errors that were quickly corrected.	Not applicable.	**0** Any information presented was not correct.	
Prop Did the speaker have at least one prop that was directly related to the presentation?	**20** Presenter had a prop and it complemented the presentation.	**12** Presenter had a prop, but it was not the best choice.	**4** Presenter had a prop, but there was no clear reason for it.	**0** Presenter had no prop.	
Content Consistent Did the speaker stay on topic?	**10** Presenter stayed on topic 100% of the time.	**7** Presenter stayed on topic 90%–99% of the time.	**4** Presenter stayed on topic 80%–89% of the time.	**0** It was hard to tell what the topic was.	
Flow Was the speaker familiar and comfortable with the material so that it flowed well?	**10** Presentation flowed well. Speaker did not stumble over words.	**7** Presenter had some flow problems, but they did not distract from information.	**4** Some flow problems interrupted the presentation, and presenter seemed flustered.	**0** Constant flow problems occurred, and information was not presented so that it could be understood.	
				Total Grade:	

Figure 4.3. Student presentation rubric.

Topic: _____		**Student's Name:** _____

On a scale of 1–10, rate the following areas:

Content (How in depth was the information? How well did the speaker know the information? Was the information correct? Could the speaker answer questions?)		Give one short reason why you gave this number.
Flow (Did the presentation flow smoothly? Did the speaker appear confident and ready to speak?)		Give one short reason why you gave this number.
Prop (Did the speaker explain his or her prop? Did this choice seem logical? Was it the best choice?)		Give one short reason why you gave this number.

Comments: Below, write two things that you think the presenter did well:

1.

2.

Topic: _____		**Student's Name:** _____

On a scale of 1–10, rate the following areas:

Content (How in depth was the information? How well did the speaker know the information? Was the information correct? Could the speaker answer questions?)		Give one short reason why you gave this number.
Flow (Did the presentation flow smoothly? Did the speaker appear confident and ready to speak?)		Give one short reason why you gave this number.
Prop (Did the speaker explain his or her prop? Did this choice seem logical? Was it the best choice?)		Give one short reason why you gave this number.

Comments: Below, write two things that you think the presenter did well:

1.

2.

Figure 4.4. Student feedback form.

The Menus

The stories, novels, and poems that have been selected for inclusion in this book are found on the list of text exemplars in Appendix B of the Common Core State Standards for English Language Arts, which can be accessed at http://www.corestandards.org/assets/Appendix_B.pdf.

How to Use the Menu Pages

Each menu in this section has:
- an introduction page for the teacher;
- a highly modified menu, indicated by a triangle (▲) in the upper right hand corner;
- a moderately modified menu, indicated by a circle (●) in the upper right hand corner;
- an unmodified, advanced menu, indicated by a square (■) in the upper right hand corner; and
- any specific activities mentioned on the menus.

Introduction Pages

The introduction pages are meant to provide an overview of each menu. They are divided into various areas.

1. *Title and Menu Type.* The top of each introductory page will note the title of the story, novel, or poem as well as the menu type(s) used. Each novel included has three menus, a highly modified menu (▲), a slightly modified/on-level menu (●), and an advanced menu (■). When possible, all three menus are in the same format, however, sometimes in order to modify for special needs students, the lowest level menu may have a different format to control the amount of choice a student faces at one time. The Poetry Shape menus cover all three levels within one menu.

2. *Brief Synopsis.* Under the title of the menu, a brief synopsis of the text has been included for teacher reference.

3. *Objectives Covered Through the Menu and Activities.* This area will list all of the objectives that the menu can address. Menus are arranged in such a way that if students complete the guidelines set forth in the menu's instructions, all of these objectives will be covered. Some objectives may be designated with a shape at the end, which indicates that the specific objective is only addressed on its corresponding menu.

4. *Materials Needed by Students for Completion.* The introduction page includes a list of materials that may be needed by students as they complete either menu. Any materials listed that are used in only **one** of the three menus are designated with that menu's corresponding shape code. Students do have the choice in the menu items they would like to complete, so it is possible that the teacher will not need all of these materials for every student. In addition to any materials listed for specific menus, it is expected that the teacher will provide, or students will have access to, the following materials for each menu:
    a. lined paper;
    b. blank 8 1/2" by 11" white paper;
    c. glue; and
    d. crayons, colored pencils, or markers.

5. *Special Notes on the Modifications of These Menus.* Some menu formats have special management issues or considerations when it comes to modifying for different ability levels. This section will review additional options available for modifying each menu.

6. *Special Notes on the Use of This Menu.* Some menus allow students to present demonstrations, experiments, songs, or PowerPoint presentations to their classmates. This section will provide any special tips on managing products that may require more time, supplies, or space. This section will also share any tips to consider for a specific activity.

7. *Time Frame.* Each menu has its own ideal time frame based on its structure, but all work best with at least a one-week time frame. Menus that assess more objectives are better suited to more than 2 weeks. This section will give you an overview about the best time frame for completing the entire menu, as well as options for shorter time periods. If teachers do not have time to devote to an entire menu, they certainly can choose the 1–2-day option for any menu topic students are currently studying.

8. *Suggested Forms.* This is a list of the rubrics, templates, or reproducibles that should be available for students as the menus are introduced and completed. If a menu has a free-choice option, the appropriate proposal form also will be listed here.

CHAPTER 5

Novels, Short Stories, and Drama

The Odyssey

20-50-80 Menu

Reading Objectives Covered Through These Menus and These Activities

- Students will represent textual evidence and use it to prove conclusions.
- Students will make and explain inferences made from the story.
- Students will make predictions based on what is read.
- Students will represent textual evidence by using story maps.
- Students will analyze characters, their relationships, and their importance in the story.
- Students will recognize and analyze story plot and problem resolution.

Writing Objectives Covered Through These Menus and These Activities

- Students will write to express their feelings, inform, explain, describe, narrate, influence, persuade, reflect, or problem solve.
- Students will support their responses with textual evidence.

Materials Needed by Students for Completion

- *The Odyssey* by Homer
- Poster board or large white paper
- Materials for board games (folders, colored cards, etc.)
- *The Odyssey* Cube template ▲
- Story map ▲ ●
- Blank index cards (for trading cards)
- Scrapbooking materials

Special Notes on the Modifications of These Menus

- If needed, further modifications can be made to a 20-50-80 menu based on the needs of your students. The easiest modification is altering the point goal from 100; lowering or raising the goal on a menu by 10 (or 20) points is appropriate if additional modification up or down is needed.

Time Frame

- 1–2 weeks—Students are given a menu as the unit is started, and the teacher discusses all of the product options on the menu. As the different options are discussed, students will choose the activities they are most interested in completing so they meet their goal of 100 points. As the lessons progress through the week(s), the teacher and students refer back to the menu options associated with the content being taught.

- 1–2 days—The teacher chooses an activity or product from the menu to use with the entire class.

Suggested Forms

- All-purpose rubric
- Student presentation rubric
- Proposal form for point-based projects

The Odyssey

Directions: Choose at least two activities from the options below. The activities must total 100 points. Place a checkmark next to each box to show which activities you will complete. All activities must be completed by: _____.

20 points

❏ Complete a story map for *The Odyssey*.

❏ Complete a story cube for *The Odyssey*.

50 points

❏ Design a set of trading cards for the different characters Odysseus meets in *The Odyssey*.

❏ Create a board game that allows players to experience Odysseus's adventures during *The Odyssey*.

❏ Create a folded quiz book that quizzes your classmates on *The Odyssey*.

❏ Free choice: Submit a proposal form for a product of your choice.

80 points

❏ Design a graphic novel that details the adventures found in *The Odyssey*.

❏ Develop a scrapbook that Odysseus could use to document his adventures.

The Odyssey

Directions: Choose at least two activities from the options below. The activities must total 100 points. Place a checkmark next to each box to show which activities you will complete. All activities must be completed by: _____.

20 points

❑ Design a set of trading cards for the different characters who have an impact on Odysseus's adventures in *The Odyssey*.

❑ Complete a story map for *The Odyssey*.

50 points

❑ Create a board game that allows players to experience Odysseus's adventures during *The Odyssey*.

❑ Create a folded quiz book that quizzes your classmates on quotes from *The Odyssey*. Your questions should focus on who said the quote as well as why it is important to the story.

❑ Design a graphic novel that details Penelope's experiences during *The Odyssey*.

❑ Free choice: Submit a proposal form for a product of your choice.

80 points

❑ Although Odysseus had many varied experiences in his travels, determine the adventure that includes the best example of Odysseus displaying his heroic traits. Create a You Be the Person Presentation in which you come to class as Odysseus. Be ready to discuss this adventure and the way you used your cunning.

❑ Develop a scrapbook that Odysseus could share with Penelope that documents the important aspects of his travels. Decorate each page using a theme appropriate to that adventure.

The Odyssey

Directions: Choose at least two activities from the options below. The activities must total 100 points. Place a checkmark next to each box to show which activities you will complete. All activities must be completed by: _____.

20 points

❏ Design a set of trading cards for the different characters who have an impact on Odysseus's adventures *The Odyssey*.

❏ Write an obituary for an important character who dies during *The Odyssey*.

50 points

❏ Create a board game that allows players to experience Odysseus's adventures during *The Odyssey*.

❏ Develop a scrapbook for Odysseus and his travels. Be sure and decorate each page using a theme appropriate to that adventure.

❏ Design a class game that quizzes your classmates on the plot developments, characters, and their traits found in *The Odyssey*. Be sure to include a Who Said It? round in which your classmates have to guess which character said each quote that is read.

❏ Free choice: Submit a proposal form for a product of your choice.

80 points

❏ *The Odyssey* is a tale filled with many short adventures. Choose the adventure that you think best illustrates Odysseus' heroic traits and create a children's book for this adventure.

❏ Although Odysseus had many varied experiences in his travels, determine the adventure that includes the best example of Odysseus displaying his cunning and problem-solving skills. Create a You Be the Person Presentation in which you come to class as Odysseus. Be ready to discuss this adventure and the way you used your cunning.

The *Odyssey* Cube

Use the cube on the left to share the different aspects of *The Odyssey*.

You may use this template or design your own cube.

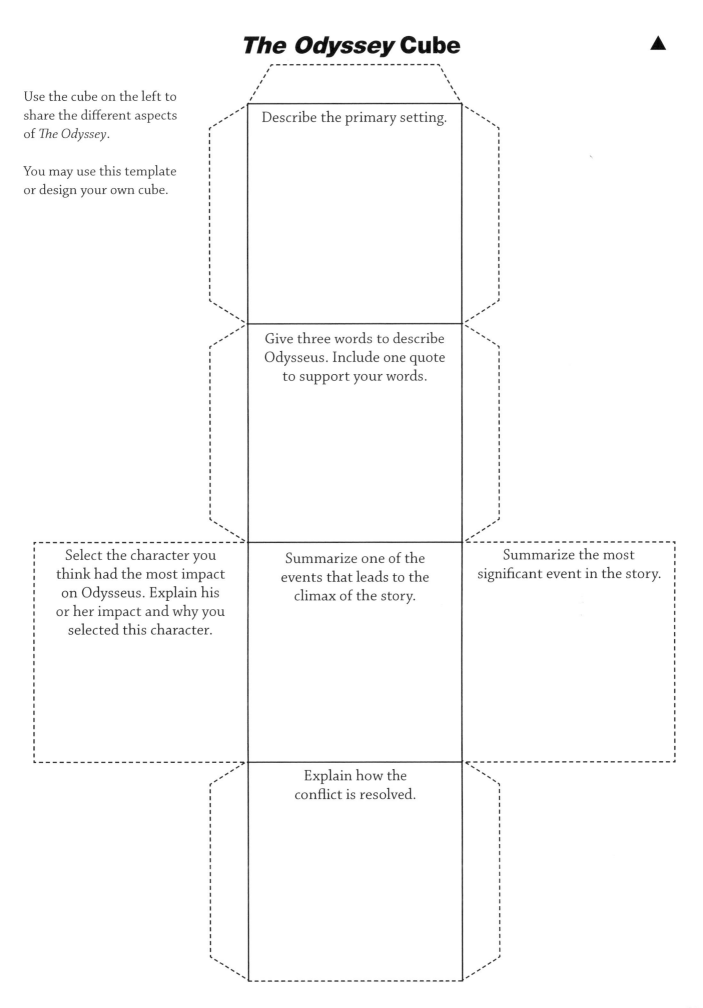

Describe the primary setting.

Give three words to describe Odysseus. Include one quote to support your words.

Select the character you think had the most impact on Odysseus. Explain his or her impact and why you selected this character.

Summarize one of the events that leads to the climax of the story.

Summarize the most significant event in the story.

Explain how the conflict is resolved.

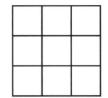

Fahrenheit 451

Meal Menu ▲ and
Tic-Tac-Toe Menu ● ■

Reading Objectives Covered Through These Menus and These Activities

- Students will represent textual evidence and use it to prove conclusions.
- Students will make and explain inferences made from the story.
- Students will analyze the various literary aspects of a story.
- Students will represent textual evidence by using story maps.
- Students will analyze characters, their relationships, and their importance in the story.
- Students will recognize and analyze story plot and problem resolution.

Writing Objectives Covered Through These Menus and These Activities

- Students will write to express their feelings, inform, explain, describe, narrate, entertain, influence, persuade, reflect, or problem solve.
- Students will support their responses with textual evidence.

Materials Needed by Students for Completion

- *Fahrenheit 451* by Ray Bradbury
- Poster board or large white paper
- DVD or VHS recorder (for videos, commercials, news reports ▲)
- Blank index cards (trading cards, mobiles) ▲
- Recycled materials for museum exhibit ● ■
- Coat hangers (for mobiles) ▲
- String (for mobiles) ▲
- Story map ▲
- Microsoft PowerPoint or other slideshow software ■
- Magazines (for collages) ●
- "Dover Beach"by Matthew Arnold (see p. 65) ■
- Scrapbooking materials ■

Special Notes on the Modifications of These Menus

- This topic has two different menu formats: The Meal menu (▲) and Tic-Tac-Toe (●) menu. The Meal menu is specifically selected for the triangle ▲ option as it easily allows the menu to be broken into manageable bits; the different meals separate the page, making it less daunting for special needs students. The space between the meals makes it easy for the teacher to cut the menu as needed based on the comfort level of the students. If it is the first time choice is being introduced, then the children may receive only the strip of the top breakfast options. Then, when they have finished one of those options, they can receive a strip of lunches and finally, the enrichment-level dinner and dessert activities. After students have grown more accustomed to making choices, the menu might be cut just once after the lunch options, so students can select a breakfast and a lunch and submit them to the teacher. Then, they can choose from the dinner strip they receive. The ultimate goal would be for students to have all nine options at once and not be overwhelmed.

Special Notes on the Use of These Menus

- These menus give students the opportunity to create a recorded video, whether it is a simple video, a commercial, or a news report ▲. Although students enjoy producing their own videos, there often are difficulties obtaining the equipment and scheduling the use of a video recorder. This activity can be modified by allowing students to act out the product (like a play) or, if students have the technology, allowing them to produce a webcam version of their presentation.

- The circle and square menus ● ■ ask students to use recycled materials to create their museum exhibit. This does not mean only plastic and paper; instead, students should focus on using materials in new ways. It works well if a box is started for "recycled" contributions at the beginning of the school year. That way, students always have access to these types of materials.

Time Frame

- 2–3 weeks—Students are given the menu as the unit is started. As the teacher presents lessons throughout the week, he or she should refer back to the menu options associated with that content. The teacher will go over all of the options for that content and have students place check marks in the boxes that represent the activities they are most interested in completing. As students choose activities, they should complete a column or a row. When students complete this pattern, they have completed one activity from each content area, learning style, or level of Bloom's revised taxonomy, depending on the design of the menu.

- 1 week—At the start of the unit, the teacher chooses the three activities he or she feels are most valuable for students. Stations can be set up in the classroom. These three activities are available for student choice throughout the week as regular instruction takes place.

- 1–2 days—The teacher chooses an activity from the menu to use with the entire class.

Suggested Forms

- All-purpose rubric
- Student presentation rubric
- Free-choice proposal form

Dover Beach

by Matthew Arnold

The sea is calm tonight.
The tide is full, the moon lies fair
Upon the straits;—on the French coast the light
Gleams and is gone; the cliffs of England stand,
Glimmering and vast, out in the tranquil bay.
Come to the window, sweet is the night-air!

Only, from the long line of spray
Where the sea meets the moon-blanched land,
Listen! you hear the grating roar
Of pebbles which the waves draw back, and fling.
At their return, up the high strand,
Begin, and cease, and then again begin,
With tremulous cadence slow, and bring
The eternal note of sadness in.

Sophocles long ago
Heard it on the Aegean, and it brought
Into his mind the turbid ebb and flow
Of human misery; we
Find also in the sound a thought,
Hearing it by this distant northern sea.

The Sea of Faith
Was once, too, at the full, and round earth's shore
Lay like the folds of a bright girdle furled.
But now I only hear
Its melancholy, long, withdrawing roar,
Retreating, to the breath
Of the night-wind, down the vast edges drear
And naked shingles of the world.

Ah, love, let us be true
To one another! for the world, which seems
To lie before us like a land of dreams,
So various, so beautiful, so new,
Hath really neither joy, nor love, nor light,
Nor certitude, nor peace, nor help for pain;
And we are here as on a darkling plain
Swept with confused alarms of struggle and flight,
Where ignorant armies clash by night.

Fahrenheit 451

Directions: Choose one activity each for breakfast, lunch, and dinner. Dessert is an activity you can choose to do after you have finished your other meals. All products must be completed by: _____.

Breakfast

❑ Record a video in which you describe the characters found in this story.

❑ Make a set of trading cards for the different characters in *Fahrenheit 451*.

❑ Make a mobile of important quotes about *Fahrenheit 451* characters. Explain each quote.

Lunch

❑ Complete a story map for *Fahrenheit 451*.

❑ Build a three-dimensional timeline for the events that take place in our story.

❑ Design a new book cover for *Fahrenheit 451*.

Dinner

❑ Make a poster-sized Venn diagram that compares and contrasts our society to Montag's.

❑ Research the banning of books. Prepare a video about why books are being banned in our country.

❑ Free choice: Submit a free choice proposal that compares our society and Montag's.

Dessert

❑ Create a commercial that could be used to recruit firemen. Be sure and include information about the job and its role in society.

❑ Record a news report that shares the story of the old woman ("The Hearth and the Salamander") and her desire to not be separated from her books.

Fahrenheit 451

Directions: Check the boxes you plan to complete. They should form a tic-tac-toe across or down. All products are due by: _____.

☐ **What About Us?**	☐ **We Need You!**	☐ **Saying It With Song**
Make a poster-sized Venn diagram that compares and contrasts our society and Montag's. Include quotes from the novel to support your statements about Montag's society.	Create a commercial that could be used to recruit firemen. Be sure and include important information about the job and its role in society.	Select a song (could be well known or obscure) that could be meaningful as Montag examines his thoughts throughout the story. Share the song and tell how it relates to Montag's life and decisions he makes in *Fahrenheit 451*.
☐ **The Offender**	☐ **Free Choice: *On Montag's society*** (Fill out your proposal form before beginning the free choice!)	☐ **Banned Books**
Write a newspaper article that shares the story of the old woman ("The Hearth and the Salamander") and her desire to not be separated from her books.		Research the banning of books. Prepare a video about why books are being banned in our country. Compare our reasons for banning with those found in *Fahrenheit 451*.
☐ **A Few Simple Questions**	☐ **The Book of Ecclesiastes**	☐ **What About Us?**
Consider the questions Clarisse asks Montag, as well as her observations about those around her. Record a video diary in which Clarisse talks about her encounters with Montag.	Select a verse from the Book of Ecclesiastes that you feel would be most meaningful to Montag. Design a collage with the verse as well as pictures and words that support its meaning.	Revisit the history Beatty provides for the beginning of the burning of books. Build a museum exhibit that shares how Montag's society began the book burning process.

Name: _____

Fahrenheit 451

Directions: Check the boxes you plan to complete. They should form a tic-tac-toe across or down. All products are due by: _____.

What About Us? Prepare a PowerPoint presentation that shares the similarities between our society and Montag's. Include examples from current events and recent history as well as quotes from the novel.	**We Need You!** Create a commercial that could be used to recruit firemen. Be sure and include quotes from Beatty about the position as well as important information about the job and its role in society.	**"Dover Beach"** Read "Dover Beach" by Matthew Arnold. Make a poster that shows the poem "Dover Beach" and how each line of the poem relates to Montag's life and experiences at that moment. Include quotes from the novel to support your analogies.
The Offender Write a newspaper article that shares the story of the old woman ("The Hearth and the Salamander") and her desire to not be separated from her books.	**Free Choice:** ***On Montag's society*** (Fill out your proposal form before beginning the free choice!)	**Banned Books** Research the banning of books. Prepare a video that discusses what kinds of books are being banned in our society, as well as the reasons for their banning. Share your opinion on this action and how it relates to *Fahrenheit 451*.
The Book of Ecclesiastes Design a scrapbook of quotes from the book that Montag has been given the responsibility to memorize. For each quote, include an analysis of how it relates to the society of *Fahrenheit 451*.	**A Few Simple Questions** Consider the questions Clarisse asks Montag, as well as her observations about the world around her. Write a journal that Clarisse may have kept detailing her encounters with Montag with her last entry being the day of her accident.	**What About Us?** Revisit the history Beatty provides for the origin of the book burning. Build a museum exhibit that shares how our society parallels Montag's and the dangers of this similarity.

The Grapes of Wrath

List Menu

Reading Objectives Covered Through These Menus and These Activities

- Students will represent textual evidence and use it to prove conclusions.
- Students will make and explain inferences made from the story.
- Students will analyze the various literary aspects of a story.
- Students will represent textual evidence by using story maps.
- Students will analyze characters, their relationships, and their importance in the story.
- Students will recognize and analyze story plot and problem resolution.

Writing Objectives Covered Through These Menus and These Activities

- Students will write to express their feelings, inform, explain, describe, narrate, entertain, persuade, reflect, or problem solve.
- Students will support their responses with textual evidence.
- Students will exhibit voice in their writing.

Materials Needed by Students for Completion

- *The Grapes of Wrath* by John Steinbeck
- Poster board or large white paper
- United States road map
- Graph paper or Internet access (for crossword puzzles) ▲ ●
- Magazines (for collages) ▲
- Story map
- Recycled materials (for museum exhibit, puppets ▲)
- DVD or VHS recorder (for news reports ▲, videos ● ■)
- Socks (for puppets) ▲
- Paper bags (for puppets) ▲
- Microsoft PowerPoint or other slideshow software ● ■

Special Notes on the Modifications of These Menus

- Because a List menu is a point-based menu, it is easy to provide additional modifications by simply changing the point goal for those students who need it. The bottom of the menu has a short contract that can be used to record any changes. The two-page format of the triangle ▲ and circle ● menus also allow for additional modification by mixing and matching the pages.

The front of each of these two-page menus has the lower and middle-level activities, while the second page has the higher level activities and contract. Additional modifications can be made by using the first page from the circle menu ● with the second page from the triangle menu ▲. This will allow students a little more flexibility when approaching the higher level activities.

Special Notes on the Use of These Menus

- These menus give students the opportunity to create a video or news report ▲. Although students enjoy producing their own videos, there often are difficulties obtaining the equipment and scheduling the use of a video recorder. This activity can be modified by allowing students to act out the product (like a play) or, if students have the technology, allowing them to produce a webcam version of their presentation.
- These menus ask students to use recycled materials to create their museum exhibit. This does not mean only plastic and paper; instead, students should focus on using materials in new ways. It works well if a box is started for "recycled" contributions at the beginning of the school year. That way, students always have access to these types of materials.

Time Frame

- 1–2 weeks—Students are given the menu as the unit is started, and the guidelines and point expectations are discussed. Students usually will need to earn 100 points for 100%, although there is an opportunity for extra credit if the teacher would like to use another target number. Because this menu covers one topic in depth, the teacher will go over all of the options for the topic being covered and have students place check marks in the boxes next to the activities they are most interested in completing. Teachers will need to set aside a few moments to sign the agreement at the bottom of the page with each student. As instruction continues, activities are completed by students and submitted to the teacher for grading.
- 1–2 days—The teacher chooses an activity or product from an objective to use with the entire class during that lesson time.

Suggested Forms

- All-purpose rubric
- Student presentation rubric
- Proposal form for point-based products

The Grapes of Wrath: Side 1

Guidelines:

1. You may complete as many of the activities listed within the time period.
2. You may choose any combination of activities.
3. Your goal is 100 points. You may earn up to _____ points extra credit.
4. You may be as creative as you like within the guidelines listed below.
5. You must show your plan to your teacher by _____.
6. Activities may be turned in at any time during the working time period. They will be graded and recorded on this sheet as you continue to work, so keep it safe!

Plan to Do	Activity to Complete (Side 1: 10–25 points)	Point Value	Date Completed	Points Earned
	Using a United States road map, highlight the route that the Joads took as they traveled across the country.	10		
	Complete another student's crossword puzzle.	15		
	Create a crossword puzzle for key vocabulary words found in this story.	15		
	Create an acrostic for the word *family*. Use words and phrases from *The Grapes of Wrath* for each letter.	15		
	Design a collage of words that represents the tone and mode of this story.	15		
	Complete a story map for *The Grapes of Wrath*.	20		
	Design a new book cover for *The Grapes of Wrath*.	20		
	On a poster, create a map that shows all of the places discussed in the story. Include a quote about each place.	20		
	Design an advertisement that Floyd Knowles could have posted to motivate others to join his cause.	25		
	Total number of points you are planning to earn from Side 1.	**Total points earned from Side 1:**		

The Grapes of Wrath: Side 2

Guidelines:

1. You may complete as many of the activities listed within the time period.
2. You may choose any combination of activities.
3. Your goal is 100 points. You may earn up to _____ points extra credit.
4. You may be as creative as you like within the guidelines listed below.
5. You must show your plan to your teacher by _____.
6. Activities may be turned in at any time during the working time period. They will be graded and recorded on this sheet as you continue to work, so keep it safe!

Plan to Do	Activity to Complete (Side 2: 25–35 points)	Point Value	Date Completed	Points Earned
	Complete a Venn diagram to compare and contrast modern-day migrant workers with the workers in *The Grapes of Wrath*.	25		
	Prepare a poster with photos from this time period to illustrate the people and the conditions they experienced.	25		
	Build a museum exhibit that could be used in a present-day museum to teach others about migrant workers.	30		
	Create an obituary that could be used for one of the characters who dies in the book.	30		
	Make a news report that covers the events in Chapter 26.	30		
	Create a puppet for the character who you feel has changed the most in this story. Have your puppet talk about these changes.	30		
	Prepare a research paper that addresses the reasons behind The Great Depression and its impact on different areas of the United States.	35		
	Pretend you are a newspaper reporter who is reporting on the conditions of the migrant workers during this time period. Write a newspaper article that details your findings. Include an interview with one of the characters using quotes from the story.	35		
	Write another chapter to this book that shares what happens to the characters after the end of the novel.	35		
	Free choice: Submit your free choice proposal form for a product of your choice.			
	Total number of points you are planning to earn from Side 1.	**Total points earned from Side 1:**		
	Total number of points you are planning to earn from Side 2.	**Total points earned from Side 2:**		
		Grand Total (/100)		

I am planning to complete _____ activities that could earn up to a total of _____ points.

Teacher's initials _____ Student's signature _____

The Grapes of Wrath: Side 1

Guidelines:

1. You may complete as many of the activities listed within the time period.
2. You may choose any combination of activities.
3. Your goal is 100 points. You may earn up to _____ points extra credit.
4. You may be as creative as you like within the guidelines listed below.
5. You must show your plan to your teacher by _____.
6. Activities may be turned in at any time during the working time period. They will be graded and recorded on this sheet as you continue to work, so keep it safe!

Plan to Do	Activity to Complete (Side 1: 10–20 points)	Point Value	Date Completed	Points Earned
	Complete another student's crossword puzzle.	10		
	Create an acrostic for the word *family*. Use words and phrases for each letter that show how "family" is one of the themes in *The Grapes of Wrath*.	10		
	Using a United States road map, highlight the route that the Joads took as they traveled across the country.	10		
	Complete a story map for *The Grapes of Wrath*.	15		
	Create a crossword puzzle for key vocabulary words found in this story.	15		
	Complete a Venn diagram to compare and contrast modern-day migrant workers with the workers in *The Grapes of Wrath*.	20		
	Create a three facts and a fib about the significance of this novel's title.	20		
	Design an advertisement that Floyd Knowles could have posted to motivate others to join his cause.	20		
	On a poster, create a map that shows all of the places discussed in the story. Include a quote about each place.	20		
	Total number of points you are planning to earn from Side 1.	**Total points earned from Side 1:**		

Name: _____

The Grapes of Wrath: Side 2

Guidelines:

1. You may complete as many of the activities listed within the time period.
2. You may choose any combination of activities.
3. Your goal is 100 points. You may earn up to _____ points extra credit.
4. You may be as creative as you like within the guidelines listed below.
5. You must show your plan to your teacher by _____.
6. Activities may be turned in at any time during the working time period. They will be graded and recorded on this sheet as you continue to work, so keep it safe!

Plan to Do	Activity to Complete (Side 2: 25–30 points)	Point Value	Date Completed	Points Earned
	Build a museum exhibit that could be used in a present-day museum to teach others about what migrant workers experienced during this time period.	25		
	Create a PowerPoint presentation of photos from this time period to illustrate the people and the conditions they experienced.	25		
	Create an obituary that could be used for one of the characters who dies in the book.	25		
	Record a video that discusses your opinion of Tom's actions in Chapter 26.	25		
	Keep a diary with at least seven entries for Rose of Sharon that details her experiences from her move to California to the final event in the book.	30		
	Prepare a research paper that addresses the reasons behind The Great Depression and its impact on different areas of the United States.	30		
	Pretend you are a newspaper reporter who is reporting on the conditions of the migrant workers during this time period. Write a newspaper article that details your findings. Include an interview with one of the characters using quotes from the story.	30		
	Write another chapter to this book that shares what happens to the characters after the end of the novel.	30		
	Free choice: Submit your free choice proposal form for a product of your choice.			
	Total number of points you are planning to earn from Side 1.	**Total points earned from Side 1:**		
	Total number of points you are planning to earn from Side 2.	**Total points earned from Side 2:**		
		Grand Total (/100)		

I am planning to complete _____ activities that could earn up to a total of _____ points.

Teacher's initials _____ Student's signature _____

The Grapes of Wrath

Guidelines:

1. You may complete as many of the activities listed within the time period.
2. You may choose any combination of activities.
3. Your goal is 100 points. You may earn up to _____ points extra credit.
4. You may be as creative as you like within the guidelines listed below.
5. You must show your plan to your teacher by _____.
6. Activities may be turned in at any time during the working time period. They will be graded and recorded on this sheet as you continue to work, so keep it safe!

Plan to Do	Activity to Complete	Point Value	Date Completed	Points Earned
	Create an acrostic for the word *family*. Use words and phrases for each letter that show how "family" is one of the themes in *The Grapes of Wrath*.	10		
	Complete a story map for *The Grapes of Wrath*.	15		
	Complete a Venn diagram to compare and contrast modern-day migrant workers with the workers in *The Grapes of Wrath*.	15		
	Create a three facts and a fib about the significance of this novel's title.	15		
	Build a museum exhibit that could be used in a present-day museum to teach others about what the Joad family and others like them experienced during this time period.	20		
	Create a PowerPoint presentation of photos from this time period to illustrate the people and the conditions they experienced.	20		
	Design an advertisement that Floyd Knowles could have posted to motivate others to join his cause.	20		
	On a poster, create a map that shows all of the places discussed in the story. Include a quote about each place as well as a present-day fact about the location.	20		
	Create an obituary that could be used for one of the characters who dies in the book.	25		
	Keep a diary with at least 10 entries for Rose of Sharon that details her experiences from her move to California to the final event in the book.	25		
	Prepare a research paper that addresses the reasons behind The Great Depression and its impact on different areas of the United States.	25		
	Pretend you are a newspaper reporter who is reporting on the conditions of the migrant workers during this time period. Write a newspaper article that details your findings. Include an interview with one of the characters using quotes from the story.	25		
	Record a video in which you support or condemn Tom's actions in Chapter 26.	25		
	Write another chapter to this book that provides insight into the fates of the characters in the barn at the end of the novel.	30		
	Free choice: Submit your free choice proposal form for a product of your choice.			
	Total number of points you are planning to earn.	**Total points earned:**		

I am planning to complete _____ activities that could earn up to a total of _____ points.

Teacher's initials _____ Student's signature _____

"The Gift of the Magi"

20-50-80 Menu

Reading Objectives Covered Through These Menus and These Activities

- Students will represent textual evidence and use it to prove conclusions.
- Students will make and explain inferences made from the story.
- Students will analyze the various literary aspects of a story.
- Students will analyze characters, their relationships, and their importance in the story.
- Students will recognize and analyze story plot and problem resolution.

Writing Objectives Covered Through These Menus and These Activities

- Students will write to express their feelings, inform, explain, describe, narrate, entertain, persuade, reflect, or problem solve.
- Students will exhibit voice in their writing.

Materials Needed by Students for Completion

- "The Gift of the Magi" by O. Henry
- Poster board or large white paper
- Story map ▲
- Microsoft PowerPoint or other slideshow software ■
- DVD or VHS recorder (for commercials, news reports ▲ ●)
- Magazines (for collages)

Special Notes on the Modifications of These Menus

- If needed, further modifications can be made to a 20-50-80 menu based on the needs of your students. The easiest modification is altering the point goal from 100; lowering or raising the goal on a menu by 10 (or 20) points is appropriate if additional modification up or down is needed.

Special Notes on the Use of These Menus

- These menus give students the opportunity to create a news report ▲ or commercial. Although students enjoy producing their own videos, there often are difficulties obtaining the equipment and scheduling the use of a video recorder. This activity can be modified by allowing students to act out the product (like a play) or, if students have the technology, allowing them to produce a webcam version of their presentation.

Time Frame

- 1–2 weeks—Students are given a menu as the unit is started, and the teacher discusses all of the product options on the menu. As the different options are discussed, students will choose the activities they are most interested in completing so they meet their goal of 100 points. As the lessons progress through the week(s), the teacher and students refer back to the menu options associated with the content being taught.
- 1–2 days—The teacher chooses an activity or product from the menu to use with the entire class.

Suggested Forms

- All-purpose rubric
- Student presentation rubric
- Proposal form for point-based projects

"The Gift of the Magi"

Directions: Choose at least two activities from the options below. The activities must total 100 points. Place a checkmark next to each box to show which activities you will complete. All activities must be completed by: _____.

20 points

☐ Create a collage of items you would buy for your friends and family if you could afford them. Label each with the person's name.

☐ Retell "The Gift of the Magi" in your own words.

50 points

☐ Complete a story map for "The Gift of the Magi."

☐ Create a folded quiz book about the story elements found in "The Gift of the Magi."

☐ Brainstorm at least five different things you could do to afford to buy a gift for others. Present your ideas on a poster.

☐ Free choice: Submit a proposal form for a product of your choice.

80 points

☐ Create a commercial about the true meaning of gift giving.

☐ You are a news reporter who has just heard about the Young couple. Prepare a news report to share the importance of their gifts.

Name: _____

"The Gift of the Magi"

Directions: Choose at least two activities from the options below. The activities must total 100 points. Place a checkmark next to each box to show which activities you will complete. All activities must be completed by: _____.

20 points

☐ Create a collage of items you would buy for your friends and family if you could afford them. Label each with the person's name and why they should have that gift.

☐ Create a folded quiz book about the story elements found in "The Gift of the Magi."

50 points

☐ Write a children's book that uses the message in this book to teach younger children about the real meaning behind giving (and receiving) gifts.

☐ You are a news reporter who has just heard about the Young couple. Prepare a news report to share the importance of their gifts.

☐ Brainstorm at least eight different things you could do to afford to buy a gift for others. Rank your ideas from easiest to hardest and present your ideas on a poster.

☐ Free choice: Submit a proposal form for a product of your choice.

80 points

☐ Using the message in "The Gift of the Magi," create a commercial about the true meaning of gift giving.

☐ Write at least five journal entries from either Jim or Della's perspective as they consider and eventually decide on the gift they will give their spouse.

"The Gift of the Magi"

Directions: Choose at least two activities from the options below. The activities must total 100 points. Place a checkmark next to each box to show which activities you will complete. All activities must be completed by: _____.

20 points

- ☐ Create a collage of items you would buy for your friends and family if you could afford them. Label each with the person's name and why they should have that gift.

- ☐ Brainstorm at least 10 different things you could do to afford to buy a gift for others. Rank your ideas from easiest to hardest and present your ideas on a PowerPoint presentation.

50 points

- ☐ Write a children's book that uses the message in this book to teach younger children about the real meaning behind giving (and receiving) gifts.

- ☐ Using the message in "The Gift of the Magi," create a commercial about the true meaning of gift giving.

- ☐ Write a journal from either Jim or Della's perspective as they consider and eventually decide on the gift they will give their spouse. Include their thoughts after the gifts are given.

- ☐ Free choice: Submit a proposal form for a product of your choice.

80 points

- ☐ At the end of the story, the author indicates that Jim and Della are the Magi. Design and present a product of your choice that explains what this means and how this is true.

- ☐ This story is set in the early 1900s. Create a modern-day version of this story and perform it as a play.

To Kill a Mockingbird

List Menu

Reading Objectives Covered Through These Menus and These Activities

- Students will represent textual evidence and use it to prove conclusions.
- Students will compare one literary work with another.
- Students will make and explain inferences made from the story.
- Students will analyze the various literary aspects of a story.
- Students will represent textual evidence by using story maps.
- Students will compare different forms of a written work (written versus performed).
- Students will analyze characters, their relationships, and their importance in the story.
- Students will recognize and analyze story plot and problem resolution.

Writing Objectives Covered Through These Menus and These Activities

- Students will write to express their feelings, inform, explain, describe, narrate, entertain, persuade, reflect, or problem solve.
- Students will support their responses with textual evidence.
- Students will exhibit voice in their writing.

Materials Needed by Students for Completion

- *To Kill a Mockingbird* by Harper Lee
- Poster board or large white paper
- Magazines (for collages)
- Recycled materials (for models, dioramas ▲ ●)
- Story map ▲
- Blank index cards (for mobiles ● ■, trading cards ▲ ●)
- Coat hangers (for mobiles ● ■)
- String (for mobiles ● ■)
- Microsoft PowerPoint or other slideshow software ● ■
- Scrapbooking materials
- DVD or VHS recorder (for documentaries ● ■, videos ▲, news reports ● ■)
- Ruler (for comic strips) ● ■

Special Notes on the Modifications of These Menus

- Because a List menu is a point-based menu, it is easy to provide additional modifications by simply changing the point goal for those students who need it. The bottom of the menu has a short contract that can be used to record any changes. The two-page format of the triangle ▲ and circle ● menus also allow for additional modification by mixing and matching the pages. The front of each of these two-page menus has the lower and middle-level activities, while the second page has the higher level activities and contract. Additional modifications can be made by using the first page from the circle menu ● with the second page from the triangle menu ▲. This will allow students a little more flexibility when approaching the higher level activities.

Special Notes on the Use of These Menus

- The circle and square menus give students the opportunity to create a video ●, documentary ● ■, or news report ■. Although students enjoy producing their own videos, there often are difficulties obtaining the equipment and scheduling the use of a video recorder. This activity can be modified by allowing students to act out the product (like a play) or, if students have the technology, allowing them to produce a webcam version of their presentation.
- The triangle and circle menus ▲ ● ask students to use recycled materials to create their models and dioramas. This does not mean only plastic and paper; instead, students should focus on using materials in new ways. It works well if a box is started for "recycled" contributions at the beginning of the school year. That way, students always have access to these types of materials.

Time Frame

- 1–2 weeks—Students are given the menu as the unit is started, and the guidelines and point expectations are discussed. Students usually will need to earn 100 points for 100%, although there is an opportunity for extra credit if the teacher would like to use another target number. Because this menu covers one topic in depth, the teacher will go over all of the options for the topic being covered and have students place check marks in the boxes next to the activities they are most interested in completing. Teachers will need to set aside a few moments to sign the agreement at the bottom of the page with each student. As instruction continues, activities are completed by students and submitted to the teacher for grading.
- 1–2 days—The teacher chooses an activity or product from an objective to use with the entire class during that lesson time.

Suggested Forms

- All-purpose rubric
- Student presentation rubric
- Student-taught lesson rubric ▪
- Proposal form for point-based products

To Kill a Mockingbird: Side 1

Guidelines:

1. You may complete as many of the activities listed within the time period.
2. You may choose any combination of activities.
3. Your goal is 100 points. You may earn up to _____ points extra credit.
4. You may be as creative as you like within the guidelines listed below.
5. You must show your plan to your teacher by _____.
6. Activities may be turned in at any time during the working time period. They will be graded and recorded on this sheet as you continue to work, so keep it safe!

Plan to Do	Activity to Complete (Side 1: 15–20 points)	Point Value	Date Completed	Points Earned
	Scout and Jem found special gifts left for them in the knothole of a tree. Make a collage of gifts or surprises that someone might leave for children in present day.	15		
	Design a diorama to show the court scene in Chapter 20.	15		
	Make a poster that shares information about mockingbirds.	15		
	Complete a story map for *To Kill a Mockingbird*.	20		
	Draw a picture dictionary for at least two vocabulary words from each chapter of *To Kill a Mockingbird*.	20		
	Make character trading cards for the main characters in this story. Include at least one quote for each character.	20		
	Create a model of Maycomb. Label each house, building, or landmark with the name of the character(s) who lives there.	20		
	Make a book cover for *To Kill a Mockingbird*.	20		
	Total number of points you are planning to earn from Side 1.	**Total points earned from Side 1:**		

To Kill a Mockingbird: Side 2

Guidelines:

1. You may complete as many of the activities listed within the time period.
2. You may choose any combination of activities.
3. Your goal is 100 points. You may earn up to _____ points extra credit.
4. You may be as creative as you like within the guidelines listed below.
5. You must show your plan to your teacher by _____.
6. Activities may be turned in at any time during the working time period. They will be graded and recorded on this sheet as you continue to work, so keep it safe!

Plan to Do	Activity to Complete (Side 2: 25–35 points)	Point Value	Date Completed	Points Earned
	Design a Venn diagram that compares the city or town where you live with Maycomb. Include at least one quote from the story in your diagram.	25		
	Select a song to represent one of the characters in this story. Share the song and explain how it represents the character.	25		
	Design a scrapbook that Scout could have kept to document her experiences during the two summers in *To Kill a Mockingbird*.	30		
	Record a video that shares information about race and prejudice in the South in the 1930s.	30		
	Retell the story from Boo Radley's point of view.	30		
	Watch the movie version of this book. Write a newspaper article review to compare the two works. Be sure to note any significant events that the director left out when making the movie.	30		
	Design a children's book in which you teach others one of the life lessons that Scout learns in *To Kill a Mockingbird*.	35		
	Free choice: Submit your free choice proposal form for a product of your choice.			
	Total number of points you are planning to earn from Side 1.		**Total points earned from Side 1:**	
	Total number of points you are planning to earn from Side 2.		**Total points earned from Side 2:**	
			Grand Total (/100)	

I am planning to complete _____ activities that could earn up to a total of _____ points.

Teacher's initials _____ Student's signature _____

Name: _____   ●

To Kill a Mockingbird: Side 1

Guidelines:

1. You may complete as many of the activities listed within the time period.
2. You may choose any combination of activities.
3. Your goal is 100 points. You may earn up to _____ points extra credit.
4. You may be as creative as you like within the guidelines listed below.
5. You must show your plan to your teacher by _____.
6. Activities may be turned in at any time during the working time period. They will be graded and recorded on this sheet as you continue to work, so keep it safe!

Plan to Do	Activity to Complete (Side 1: 10–20 points)	Point Value	Date Completed	Points Earned
	Scout and Jem found special gifts left for them in the knothole of a tree. Make a collage of gifts or surprises that someone might leave for children in present day.	10		
	Create a PowerPoint presentation that shares information about mockingbirds. Include the information that Atticus shares about them in your presentation.	15		
	Design a diorama to show the court scene in Chapter 20.	15		
	Draw a picture dictionary for at least three vocabulary words from each chapter of *To Kill a Mockingbird*.	15		
	Make character trading cards for the main characters in this story. Include at least one quote for each character.	15		
	Create a model of Maycomb. Label each house, building, or landmark with the name of the character(s) who lives there.	20		
	Use a flipbook format to share character traits of the Finches' neighbors. Include at least one quote about each person.	20		
	Design a Venn diagram that compares your city or town with Maycomb.	20		
	Total number of points you are planning to earn from Side 1.	**Total points earned from Side 1:**		

Name: _____

To Kill a Mockingbird: Side 2

Guidelines:

1. You may complete as many of the activities listed within the time period.
2. You may choose any combination of activities.
3. Your goal is 100 points. You may earn up to _____ points extra credit.
4. You may be as creative as you like within the guidelines listed below.
5. You must show your plan to your teacher by _____.
6. Activities may be turned in at any time during the working time period. They will be graded and recorded on this sheet as you continue to work, so keep it safe!

Plan to Do	Activity to Complete (Side 2: 25–30 points)	Point Value	Date Completed	Points Earned
	Create a mobile that shows the works of literature referred to in this story. Provide at least one quote from each literary work mentioned.	25		
	Draw a comic strip that explains the significance of Scout and her definition of "folks."	25		
	Prepare a documentary that shares information about race and prejudice in the South in the 1930s.	25		
	Watch the movie version of this book. Write a newspaper article reviewing and comparing the two works. Be sure to note any significant events that the director left out when making the movie.	25		
	To Kill a Mockingbird has been banned from certain libraries. Record a news report that shares the reasons behind this action. Include a commentary with your thoughts on this as well.	30		
	Design a children's book in which you teach others at least two life lessons that Scout learns in *To Kill a Mockingbird*.	30		
	Design a scrapbook that Scout could have kept to document her experiences during the two summers in *To Kill a Mockingbird*.	30		
	Keep a diary of the events in this story from Boo Radley's perspective. There should be at least one entry before *To Kill a Mockingbird* begins.	30		
	Free choice: Submit your free choice proposal form for a product of your choice.			
	Total number of points you are planning to earn from Side 1.	**Total points earned from Side 1:**		
	Total number of points you are planning to earn from Side 2.	**Total points earned from Side 2:**		
		Grand Total (/100)		

I am planning to complete _____ activities that could earn up to a total of _____ points.

Teacher's initials _____ Student's signature _____

Name: _____ ■

To Kill a Mockingbird

Guidelines:

1. You may complete as many of the activities listed within the time period.
2. You may choose any combination of activities.
3. Your goal is 100 points. You may earn up to _____ points extra credit.
4. You may be as creative as you like within the guidelines listed below.
5. You must show your plan to your teacher by _____.
6. Activities may be turned in at any time during the working time period. They will be graded and recorded on this sheet as you continue to work, so keep it safe!

Plan to Do	Activity to Complete	Point Value	Date Completed	Points Earned
	Scout and Jem found special gifts left for them in the knothole of a tree. Make a collage of gifts or surprises that someone might leave for children in present day.	10		
	Use a Venn diagram to compare your town or city with Maycomb.	15		
	Create a mobile that shows the works of literature referred to in this story. Provide at least one quote for each and a brief explanation about why it was incorporated into the story.	20		
	Create a model of Maycomb. Label each house, building, or landmark with the name of the character(s) who lives there. Use a quote from the story to support where you have placed each building.	20		
	Design a scrapbook that Scout could have kept to document her experiences during the two summers in *To Kill a Mockingbird*.	20		
	Prepare a PowerPoint presentation that shares information about race and prejudice in the time period of *To Kill a Mockingbird* (1930s).	20		
	Use a flipbook to organize a character analysis of the Finches' neighbors. Include at least two quotes to support your statements about each person.	20		
	Watch the movie version of this book. Use a Venn diagram to compare the two works. Be sure to note any significant events that the director omitted from the movie.	20		
	Create a windowpane of character drawings and quotes that shows how our view of Boo Radley changes as the story progresses.	25		
	Design a children's book in which you teach others at least four life lessons that Scout learns in *To Kill a Mockingbird*.	25		
	Draw a comic strip that explains the significance of Scout and her definition of "folks."	25		
	Keep a diary of the events in this story from Boo Radley's perspective. There should be at least two entries before *To Kill a Mockingbird* begins.	25		
	To Kill a Mockingbird has been banned from certain libraries. Record a news report that shares the reasons behind this action. Include a commentary with your thoughts on this as well.	25		
	Analyze the author's portrayal of women in *To Kill a Mockingbird* based on the time period in the novel. Prepare a student-taught lesson in which you teach your classmates about your findings. Be sure to include quotes from the novel in your lesson.	30		
	Select a historical or famous figure who you believe is analogous to the symbolism of the mockingbird. Create a documentary in which you share how this figure demonstrates the intention of Harper Lee's symbolism.	30		
	Free choice: Submit your free choice proposal form for a product of your choice.			
	Total number of points you are planning to earn.		**Total points earned:**	

I am planning to complete _____ activities that could earn up to a total of _____ points.

Teacher's initials _____ Student's signature _____

The Joy Luck Club

Three-Topic List Menu

Reading Objectives Covered Through These Menus and These Activities

- Students will represent textual evidence and use it to prove conclusions.
- Students will make and explain inferences made from the story.
- Students will analyze the various literary aspects of a story.
- Students will represent textual evidence by using story maps.
- Students will analyze characters, their relationships, and their importance in the story.
- Students will recognize and analyze story plot and problem resolution.

Writing Objectives Covered Through These Menus and These Activities

- Students will write to express their feelings, inform, explain, describe, narrate, entertain, persuade, reflect, or problem solve.
- Students will support their responses with textual evidence.

Materials Needed by Students for Completion

- *The Joy Luck Club* by Amy Tan
- Poster board or large white paper
- Mahjong game ▲
- Chess game
- DVD or VHS recorder (for videos)
- Story map ▲
- *The Joy Luck Club* Cube template ▲ ●
- Scrapbooking materials ▲ ●
- Magazines (for collages) ● ■
- Blank index cards (for trading cards) ■
- Microsoft PowerPoint or other slideshow software ■
- Recycled materials (for museum exhibit) ■

Special Notes on the Modifications of These Menus

- Because a List menu is a point-based menu, it is easy to provide additional modifications by simply changing the point goal for those students who need it. The bottom of the menu has a short contract that can be used to record any changes.

Special Notes on the Use of These Menus

- These menus give students the opportunity to create a video. Although students enjoy producing their own videos, there often are difficulties obtaining the equipment and scheduling the use of a video recorder. This activity can be modified by allowing students to act out the product (like a play) or, if students have the technology, allowing them to produce a webcam version of their presentation.

- The square menu ■ asks students to use recycled materials to create their museum exhibit. This does not mean only plastic and paper; instead, students should focus on using materials in new ways. It works well if a box is started for "recycled" contributions at the beginning of the school year. That way, students always have access to these types of materials.

- The triangle menu ▲ allows students to create a bulletin board display. Some classrooms may only have one bulletin board, so the teacher can divide the board into sections, or additional classroom wall or hall space can be sectioned off for the creation of these displays. Students can plan their display based on the amount of space they are assigned.

Time Frame

- 1–2 weeks—Students are given the menu as the unit is started, and the guidelines and point expectations are discussed. Students usually will need to earn 100 points for 100%, although there is an opportunity for extra credit if the teacher would like to use another target number. Because this menu covers three topics in depth, the teacher may choose to only go over the options for the topic being covered first; the students place check marks in the boxes next to the activities they are most interested in completing. As instruction continues, additional explanation of the new topic activities can be provided. Once students have access to the entire menu, teachers will need to set aside a few moments to sign the agreement at the bottom of the page with each student. As activities are completed by students, they will be submitted to the teacher for grading.

- 1–2 days—The teacher chooses an activity or product from an objective to use with the entire class during that lesson time.

Suggested Forms

- All-purpose rubric
- Student presentation rubric
- Student-taught lesson rubric ● ■
- Proposal form for point-based products

Name: _____ ▲

The Joy Luck Club: Side 1

Guidelines:

1. You may complete as many of the activities listed as you can within the time period.
2. You may choose any combination of activities, but **must** complete at least one activity from each topic area.
3. Your goal is 100 points. You may earn up to _____ points extra credit.
4. You may be as creative as you like within the guidelines listed below.
5. You must share your plan with your teacher by _____.
6. Activities may be turned in at any time during the working time period. They will be graded and recorded on this sheet as you continue to work, so keep it safe!

Topic	Plan to Do	Activity to Complete	Point Value	Date Completed	Points Earned
Feathers From a Thousand Li Away		Using a Mahjong game, demonstrate how to play it.	15		
		Draw a timeline to share events that took place in China using Suyuan's (Jing-mei's mother) story.	20		
		Create a Venn diagram to compare and contrast the experiences of two of the women based on the stories they shared in this part of the book.	25		
		Make a bulletin board display to compare Suyuan's experience in China with a family traveling west on a wagon train.	30		
The Twenty-Six Malignant Gates		Make a mind map that shows what happens to the four women in this section.	15		
		Record a video in which you retell the parable of "The Twenty-Six Malignant Gates."	20		
		Make a flipbook to share information about Lena and Teresa Sorci's families.	25		
		Find out how to play chess. Prepare a demonstration for your classmates to share the rules of chess and how the pieces move on the board.	30		
		Total number of points you are planning to earn from Side 1.	**Total points earned from Side 1:**		

The Joy Luck Club: Side 2

Guidelines:

1. You may complete as many of the activities listed as you can within the time period.
2. You may choose any combination of activities, but **must** complete at least one activity from each topic area.
3. Your goal is 100 points. You may earn up to _____ points extra credit.
4. You may be as creative as you like within the guidelines listed below.
5. You must share your plan with your teacher by _____.
6. Activities may be turned in at any time during the working time period. They will be graded and recorded on this sheet as you continue to work, so keep it safe!

Topic	Plan to Do	Activity to Complete	Point Value	Date Completed	Points Earned
American Translation		Create a drawing that shows how the mahjong group came to be called the Joy Luck Club.	15		
		Complete a story map for *The Joy Luck Club*.	20		
		Design a scrapbook to share examples of three of the superstitions shared in this section of *The Joy Luck Club*.	25		
		Select the woman who you feel is strongest based on the stories shared in this section. Act out her story for your classmates.	30		
Queen Mother of the Western Skies		Ying-Ying says she was born in the year of the tiger, which has an impact on her nature. Make a poster that shares information about the year in which you were born.	15		
		Write a letter that Jing-mei may have written to her half sisters before going to meet them in China.	20		
		Complete *The Joy Luck Club* Cube.	25		
		Perform a song that shares the reasons why people should swallow their tears.	30		
Any		**Free choice:** Submit your free choice proposal form for a product of your choice.			
		Total number of points you are planning to earn from Side 1.	**Total points earned from Side 1:**		
		Total number of points you are planning to earn from Side 2.	**Total points earned from Side 2:**		
			Grand Total (/100)		

I am planning to complete _____ activities that could earn up to a total of _____ points.

Teacher's initials _____ Student's signature _____

Name: _____

The Joy Luck Club: Side 1

Guidelines:

1. You may complete as many of the activities listed as you can within the time period.
2. You may choose any combination of activities, but **must** complete at least one activity from each topic area.
3. Your goal is 100 points. You may earn up to _____ points extra credit.
4. You may be as creative as you like within the guidelines listed below.
5. You must share your plan with your teacher by _____.
6. Activities may be turned in at any time during the working time period. They will be graded and recorded on this sheet as you continue to work, so keep it safe!

Topic	Plan to Do	Activity to Complete	Point Value	Date Completed	Points Earned
Feathers From a Thousand Li Away		Create a poster that shows how to play the game Mahjong.	15		
		Build a three-dimensional timeline to share the historical events that took place in the 1940s in China.	20		
		Create a Venn diagram to compare and contrast the experiences of two of the women based on the stories they shared in this part of the book.	20		
		Write a story about another historic trip in which people have had to make the tough decision to leave their belongings behind.	25		
The Twenty-Six Malignant Gates		Make a mind map that shows what happens to each character in this section.	15		
		Create a collage of words and quotes to compare and contrast the lives of Lena and Teresa Sorci.	20		
		Select and read a book on chess strategies. Prepare a student-taught lesson in which you present at least one of the strategies you learned.	25		
		Record a video in which you share how the parable of "The Twenty-Six Malignant Gates" relates to two of the stories told by the girls in this section of the book.	30		
		Total number of points you are planning to earn from Side 1.	**Total points earned from Side 1:**		

Name: _____

The Joy Luck Club: Side 2

Guidelines:

1. You may complete as many of the activities listed as you can within the time period.
2. You may choose any combination of activities, but **must** complete at least one activity from each topic area.
3. Your goal is 100 points. You may earn up to _____ points extra credit.
4. You may be as creative as you like within the guidelines listed below.
5. You must share your plan with your teacher by _____.
6. Activities may be turned in at any time during the working time period. They will be graded and recorded on this sheet as you continue to work, so keep it safe!

Topic	Plan to Do	Activity to Complete	Point Value	Date Completed	Points Earned
American Translation		Create a flipbook of information for all of the people who attend Suyuan's dinner party.	15		
		Design a scrapbook to share examples of all of the superstitions shared in this section of *The Joy Luck Club*.	20		
		Write a folded quiz book that tests others on their ability to identify the women in this section by quotes they have said.	25		
		Select the woman who you feel is strongest based on the stories shared about each in this section. Write a journal with at least five entries that details the experiences that have made her stronger.	30		
Queen Mother of the Western Skies		Ying-Ying says she was born in the year of the tiger, which has an impact on her nature. Make a poster that shares information on the year in which you were born.	15		
		Complete *The Joy Luck Club* Cube.	20		
		Draw a cartoon that illustrates what Lindo and Waverly are referring to when they describe their "American face" and "Chinese face."	25		
		Write and perform a song that shares the reasons why people should swallow their tears.	30		
Any		**Free choice:** Submit your free choice proposal form for a product of your choice.			
		Total number of points you are planning to earn from Side 1.	**Total points earned from Side 1:**		
		Total number of points you are planning to earn from Side 2.	**Total points earned from Side 2:**		
			Grand Total (/100)		

I am planning to complete _____ activities that could earn up to a total of _____ points.

Teacher's initials _____ Student's signature _____

Name: _____

The Joy Luck Club

Guidelines:

1. You may complete as many of the activities listed as you can within the time period.
2. You may choose any combination of activities, but **must** complete at least one activity from each topic area.
3. Your goal is 100 points. You may earn up to _____ points extra credit.
4. You may be as creative as you like within the guidelines listed below.
5. You must share your plan with your teacher by _____.
6. Activities may be turned in at any time during the working time period. They will be graded and recorded on this sheet as you continue to work, so keep it safe!

Topic	Plan to Do	Activity to Complete	Point Value	Date Completed	Points Earned
Feathers From a Thousand Li Away		Create a poster that shows how to play the game Mahjong.	10		
		Research the events that were taking place in China in the 1940s. Prepare a museum exhibit that shares the important events and their impact on the citizens of China.	15		
		Write an essay explaining how this section's parable relates the events discussed within it.	20		
		On a poster, make a large, four-circle Venn diagram to compare and contrast the experiences of all four women based on the stories they shared in this part of the book.	25		
The Twenty-Six Malignant Gates		Make a drawing or illustration for the most significant event in this section of *The Joy Luck Club*.	10		
		Create a collage that shows how the lives of Lena and Teresa Sorci are quite different. Include quotes from the story to prove the differences.	15		
		Select and read a book on chess strategies. Prepare a student-taught lesson in which you present at least one of the strategies you learned.	20		
		Record a video in which you share how the parable of "The Twenty-Six Malignant Gates" relates to all of the stories told by the girls in this section of the book.	25		
American Translation		Create a set of trading cards for all of the people who attend Suyuan's dinner party.	10		
		Create a brochure that shares all of the superstitions shared in this section of *The Joy Luck Club*.	15		
		Create a class game in which players have to determine which of the women in this book is being described through quotes from this section and readers' observation of the character.	20		
		Select the woman who you feel is strongest based on the stories shared about each in this section. Write a journal with at least seven entries that details the experiences that have made her stronger.	25		
Queen Mother of the Western Skies		Ying-Ying says she was born in the year of the tiger, which has an impact on her nature. Research what year you were born in and create a bumper sticker that shares its qualities.	10		
		Select three songs that could be used as a soundtrack for "Queen Mother of the Western Skies." Include a paragraph explaining your choices.	15		
		Draw a cartoon that illustrates what Lindo and Waverly are referring to when they describe their "American face" and "Chinese face."	20		
		An-mei's mother shares with her the reason one should swallow his or her own tears. Do you agree? Perform a speech that shares your opinion on her reasons for doing this.	25		
Any		**Free choice**: Submit your free choice proposal form for a product of your choice.			
		Total number of points you are planning to earn.		**Total points earned:**	

I am planning to complete _____ activities that could earn up to a total of _____ points.

Teacher's initials _____ Student's signature _____

The Joy Luck Club Cube ▲ ●

Use each side of the cube to share how the lives of six of the characters in *The Joy Luck Club* could be changed if they learned the lesson that the woman in the parable learned.

Use this pattern or create your own cube. You may choose to put questions or statements on each side of your cube.

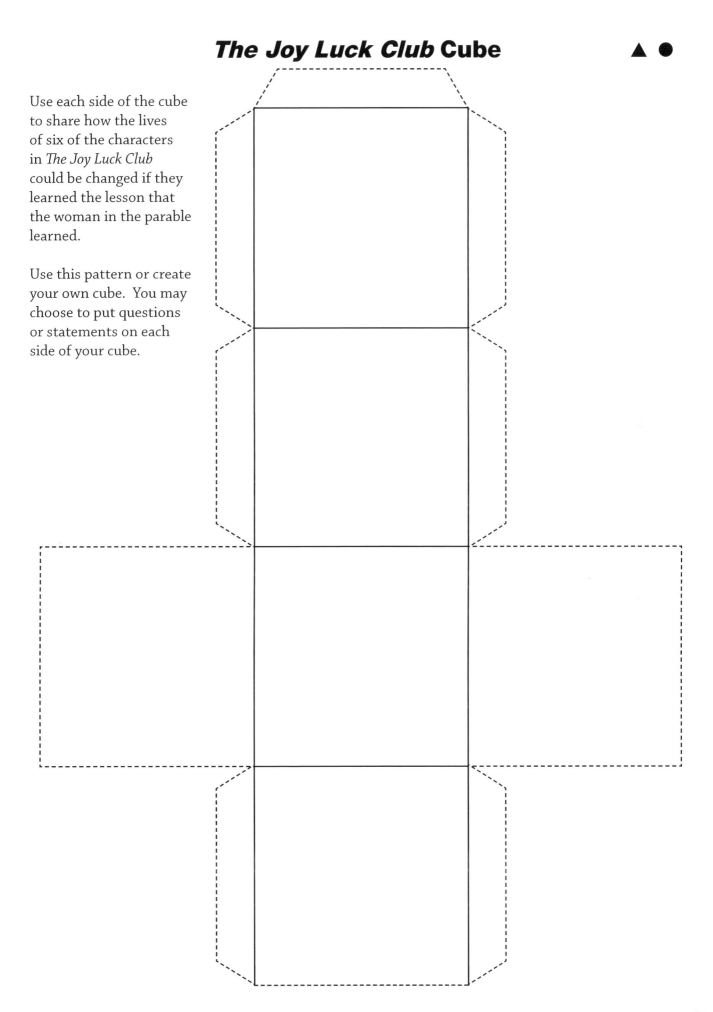

The Book Thief

List Menu

Reading Objectives Covered Through These Menus and These Activities

- Students will represent textual evidence and use it to prove conclusions.
- Students will make and explain inferences made from the story.
- Students will analyze the various literary aspects of a story.
- Students will represent textual evidence by using story maps.
- Students will analyze characters, their relationships, and their importance in the story.
- Students will recognize and analyze story plot and problem resolution.

Writing Objectives Covered Through These Menus and These Activities

- Students will write to express their feelings, inform, explain, describe, narrate, entertain, persuade, reflect, or problem solve.
- Students will support their responses with textual evidence.
- Students will exhibit voice in their writing.

Materials Needed by Students for Completion

- *The Book Thief* by Markus Zusak
- Poster board or large white paper
- Story map ▲
- Coat hangers (for mobiles) ▲
- String (for mobiles) ▲
- Blank index cards (for mobiles ▲, concentration cards ■)
- Magazines (for collages) ▲
- Scrapbooking materials
- Recycled materials (for dioramas ▲, museum exhibits)
- DVD or VHS recorder (for videos) ▲ ■
- Microsoft PowerPoint or other slideshow software ● ■

Special Notes on the Modifications of These Menus

- Because a List menu is a point-based menu, it is easy to provide additional modifications by simply changing the point goal for those students who need it. The bottom of the menu has a short contract that can be used to record any changes. The two-page format of the triangle ▲ and circle ● menus also allow for additional modification by mixing and matching the pages.

The front of each of these two-page menus has the lower and middle-level activities, while the second page has the higher level activities and contract. Additional modifications can be made by using the first page from the circle menu ● with the second page from the triangle menu ▲. This will allow students a little more flexibility when approaching the higher level activities.

Special Notes on the Use of These Menus

- The triangle ▲ and square ■ menus give students the opportunity to create a video. Although students enjoy producing their own videos, there often are difficulties obtaining the equipment and scheduling the use of a video recorder. This activity can be modified by allowing students to act out the product (like a play) or, if students have the technology, allowing them to produce a webcam version of their presentation.
- These menus ask students to use recycled materials to create their museum exhibits and dioramas ▲. This does not mean only plastic and paper; instead, students should focus on using materials in new ways. It works well if a box is started for "recycled" contributions at the beginning of the school year. That way, students always have access to these types of materials.
- The circle menu ● allows students the opportunity to create a bulletin board display. Some classrooms may only have one bulletin board, so the teacher can divide the board into sections, or additional classroom wall or hall space can be sectioned off for the creation of these displays. Students can plan their display based on the amount of space they are assigned.

Time Frame

- 1–2 weeks—Students are given the menu as the unit is started, and the guidelines and point expectations are discussed. Students usually will need to earn 100 points for 100%, although there is an opportunity for extra credit if the teacher would like to use another target number. Because this menu covers one topic in depth, the teacher will go over all of the options for the topic being covered and have students place check marks in the boxes next to the activities they are most interested in completing. Teachers will need to set aside a few moments to sign the agreement at the bottom of the page with each student. As instruction continues, activities are completed by students and submitted to the teacher for grading.
- 1–2 days—The teacher chooses an activity or product from an objective to use with the entire class during that lesson time.

Suggested Forms

- All-purpose rubric
- Student presentation rubric
- Student-taught lesson rubric ▨
- Proposal form for point-based products

The Book Thief: Side 1

Guidelines:

1. You may complete as many of the activities listed within the time period.
2. You may choose any combination of activities.
3. Your goal is 100 points. You may earn up to _____ points extra credit.
4. You may be as creative as you like within the guidelines listed below.
5. You must show your plan to your teacher by _____.
6. Activities may be turned in at any time during the working time period. They will be graded and recorded on this sheet as you continue to work, so keep it safe!

Plan to Do	Activity to Complete (Side 1: 15–20 points)	Point Value	Date Completed	Points Earned
	Make a character mobile that has cards for each character, with at least three character traits to describe each one.	15		
	Make a timeline that shares the progression of the main events in the story.	15		
	Complete a story map for *The Book Thief*.	20		
	Create a collage of words to describe the tone of *The Book Thief*.	20		
	Create a map of Molching and its surrounding areas based on information found in the story. Label the important buildings.	20		
	Make a diorama that shows how Max was hidden in the Hubermann's home.	20		
	Write an obituary for Werner.	20		
	Create a poster that shares historical information about Dachau.	20		
	Total number of points you are planning to earn from Side 1.	**Total points earned from Side 1:**		

The Book Thief: Side 2

Guidelines:

1. You may complete as many of the activities listed within the time period.
2. You may choose any combination of activities.
3. Your goal is 100 points. You may earn up to _____ points extra credit.
4. You may be as creative as you like within the guidelines listed below.
5. You must show your plan to your teacher by _____.
6. Activities may be turned in at any time during the working time period. They will be graded and recorded on this sheet as you continue to work, so keep it safe!

Plan to Do	Activity to Complete (Side 2: 25–30 points)	Point Value	Date Completed	Points Earned
	Build a museum exhibit that shares information about the Holocaust from the perspective of German people who were not Nazis.	25		
	Create a children's ABC book that shares quotes and important information from the novel.	25		
	Design a scrapbook of at least four of your favorite quotes from the story. Include who said the quote and how it relates to you or your life.	25		
	Retell your favorite part of *The Book Thief*. Be sure and explain why you liked this part the best.	25		
	Once Liesel learns to read and write, she composes letters to her mother. Write one letter that Liesel may have sent to her mother near the beginning of the story.	30		
	Prepare a presentation that shares Death's perspective on the world as he sees it. Be sure and include quotes to support your views.	30		
	Record a video that shows how Death is portrayed in *The Book Thief*.	30		
	Write and perform a song that shares the theme of beauty found throughout *The Book Thief*.	30		
	Free choice: Submit your free choice proposal form for a product of your choice.			
	Total number of points you are planning to earn from Side 1.	**Total points earned from Side 1:**		
	Total number of points you are planning to earn from Side 2.	**Total points earned from Side 2:**		
		Grand Total (/100)		

I am planning to complete _____ activities that could earn up to a total of _____ points.

Teacher's initials _____ Student's signature _____

Name: _____   ●

The Book Thief: Side 1

Guidelines:

1. You may complete as many of the activities listed within the time period.
2. You may choose any combination of activities.
3. Your goal is 100 points. You may earn up to _____ points extra credit.
4. You may be as creative as you like within the guidelines listed below.
5. You must show your plan to your teacher by _____.
6. Activities may be turned in at any time during the working time period. They will be graded and recorded on this sheet as you continue to work, so keep it safe!

Plan to Do	Activity to Complete (Side 1: 15–20 points)	Point Value	Date Completed	Points Earned
	Create a map of Molching and its surrounding areas based on information found in the story. Label the important buildings, as well as locations where certain important events take place.	15		
	Design a three-dimensional timeline that shares the progression of the main events in the story.	15		
	Select a meaningful quote from *The Book Thief* and create an illustration for it.	20		
	Create a bulletin board display to share drawings of each character, as well as a quote to describe them.	20		
	Prepare a windowpane that shares information about each book that Liesel steals throughout this story. Include a brief summary of each book.	20		
	Create a PowerPoint presentation to share historical information about the concentration camp to which Max was sent.	20		
	Write an obituary for Werner that includes information about his funeral.	20		
	Total number of points you are planning to earn from Side 1.	**Total points earned from Side 1:**		

Name: _____

The Book Thief: Side 2

Guidelines:

1. You may complete as many of the activities listed within the time period.
2. You may choose any combination of activities.
3. Your goal is 100 points. You may earn up to _____ points extra credit.
4. You may be as creative as you like within the guidelines listed below.
5. You must show your plan to your teacher by _____.
6. Activities may be turned in at any time during the working time period. They will be graded and recorded on this sheet as you continue to work, so keep it safe!

Plan to Do	Activity to Complete (Side 2: 25–30 points)	Point Value	Date Completed	Points Earned
	Build a museum exhibit that shares information about the Holocaust from the perspective of German people who were not Nazis. Include quotes from the book in your display.	25		
	Create a children's ABC book that shares symbols and important quotes from the novel.	25		
	Prepare a presentation that shares Death's perspective on the world as he sees it. Be sure and include quotes to support your views.	25		
	Design a scrapbook of at least six of your favorite quotes from the story. Include who said the quote, its importance to the character or plot, and how it relates to you or your life.	25		
	Once Liesel learns to read and write, she composes letters to her mother. Write one letter that Liesel may have sent to her mother near the beginning of the story.	25		
	Based on clues in the story, recreate one of the books that Max writes for Liesel.	25		
	Write and perform a song that shares the theme of beauty and brutality found throughout *The Book Thief*.	25		
	Write an essay that discusses how Death is portrayed in *The Book Thief*. Include a cover with a picture and quotes to support your thesis.	30		
	Free choice: Submit your free choice proposal form for a product of your choice.			
	Total number of points you are planning to earn from Side 1.		**Total points earned from Side 1:**	
	Total number of points you are planning to earn from Side 2.		**Total points earned from Side 2:**	
			Grand Total (/100)	

I am planning to complete _____ activities that could earn up to a total of _____ points.

Teacher's initials _____ Student's signature _____

Name: _____   ■

The Book Thief

Guidelines:

1. You may complete as many of the activities listed within the time period.
2. You may choose any combination of activities.
3. Your goal is 100 points. You may earn up to _____ points extra credit.
4. You may be as creative as you like within the guidelines listed below.
5. You must show your plan to your teacher by _____.
6. Activities may be turned in at any time during the working time period. They will be graded and recorded on this sheet as you continue to work, so keep it safe!

Plan to Do	Activity to Complete	Point Value	Date Completed	Points Earned
	Create a map of Molching and its surrounding areas based on information found in the story. Label the important buildings, as well as locations where certain important events take place. Label at least three real life places on your map.	15		
	Write an obituary for Werner that includes information about his funeral.	15		
	Select a meaningful quote from *The Book Thief* and create an illustration for it.	20		
	Build a museum exhibit that shares information about the Holocaust from the perspective of German people who were not Nazis. Include at least two quotes.	20		
	Create a children's ABC book that shares symbols and important quotes from the novel.	20		
	Make a Venn diagram to compare how Death presents himself in *The Book Thief* and how many people view him.	20		
	Prepare a presentation that shares Death's perspective on the world as he sees it. Be sure and include quotes to support your views.	20		
	Build a three-dimensional timeline that shows when each book is stolen and the impact each book has on Liesel's life.	20		
	Prepare a windowpane that shares information about the books that Liesel steals. Include a thoughtful drawing for each cover and a brief summary of the book's contents.	20		
	Based on clues in the story, recreate one of the books that Max writes for Liesel.	20		
	Research the concentration camp to which Max was sent. Create a PowerPoint presentation to share appropriate information about what Max may have experienced.	20		
	Create a scrapbook of at least 10 of your favorite quotes from the story. Include who said it, its importance to the novel, and how it relates to you or your life.	25		
	Create a set of concentration cards to match statements made by Death with how each statement may be perceived by the living.	25		
	Design a student-taught lesson to teach your classmates about the theme of beauty and brutality found throughout *The Book Thief*.	25		
	Liesel composes letters to her mother. Write two letters that Liesel may have sent to her mother—one at an early point in the book, one at a later point.	25		
	Write an essay that discusses how Death is portrayed in *The Book Thief*. Include a cover with a picture and quotes to support your thesis.	25		
	Select another book or story that is set in this same time period. Record a literary video that compares and contrasts the experiences of the characters in each novel.	30		
	Write a chapter for *The Book Thief* that shares what happens after Max reunites with Liesel.	30		
	Free choice: Submit your free choice proposal form for a product of your choice.			
	Total number of points you are planning to earn.		**Total points earned:**	

I am planning to complete _____ activities that could earn up to a total of _____ points.

Teacher's initials _____ Student's signature _____

Oedipus Rex

20-50-80 Menu

Reading Objectives Covered Through These Menus and These Activities

- Students will represent textual evidence and use it to prove conclusions.
- Students will make and explain inferences made from the story.
- Students will analyze the various literary aspects of a story.
- Students will analyze characters, their relationships, and their importance in the story.
- Students will recognize and analyze story plot and problem resolution.

Writing Objectives Covered Through These Menus and These Activities

- Students will write to express their feelings, inform, explain, describe, narrate, entertain, persuade, reflect, or problem solve.
- Students will support their responses with textual evidence.

Materials Needed by Students for Completion

- *Oedipus Rex* by Sophocles
- Poster board or large white paper
- Recycled materials (for dioramas) ▲
- DVD or VHS recorder (for videos) ▲ ■
- Aluminum foil (for quiz boards)
- Holiday lights (for quiz boards)
- Wires (for quiz boards)

Special Notes on the Modifications of These Menus

- If needed, further modifications can be made to a 20-50-80 menu based on the needs of your students. The easiest modification is altering the point goal from 100; lowering or raising the goal on a menu by 10 (or 20) points is appropriate if additional modification up or down is needed.

Special Notes on the Use of These Menus

- The triangle ▲ and square ■ menus give students the opportunity to create a video. Although students enjoy producing their own videos, there often are difficulties obtaining the equipment and scheduling the use of a video recorder. This activity can be modified by allowing students to act out the product (like a play) or, if students have the technology, allowing them to produce a webcam version of their presentation.

- The triangle menu ▲ asks students to use recycled materials to create their diorama. This does not mean only plastic and paper; instead, students should focus on using materials in new ways. It works well if a box is started for "recycled" contributions at the beginning of the school year. That way, students always have access to these types of materials.
- The circle ● and square ■ menus provide the opportunity for students to create a quiz board. A student-friendly informational sheet that offers the steps for constructing their own quiz board is available at http://www.cesi-science.org/attachments/article/100/QuizBoardDirections.pdf.

Time Frame

- 1–2 weeks—Students are given a menu as the unit is started, and the teacher discusses all of the product options on the menu. As the different options are discussed, students will choose the activities they are most interested in completing so they meet their goal of 100 points. As the lessons progress through the week(s), the teacher and students refer back to the menu options associated with the content being taught.
- 1–2 days—The teacher chooses an activity or product from the menu to use with the entire class.

Suggested Forms

- All-purpose rubric
- Student presentation rubric
- Proposal form for point-based projects

Oedipus Rex

Directions: Choose at least two activities from the options below. The activities must total 100 points. Place a checkmark next to each box to show which activities you will complete. All activities must be completed by: _____.

20 points

❏ Create a diorama that shows the design of the theaters in which Greek plays were performed.

❏ Make a poster on Dionysus and his relationship to the theater.

50 points

❏ Tragic heroes have both admirable traits and a flaw. Make a T-chart that identifies these characteristics in Oedipus.

❏ By answering the Riddle of the Sphinx, Oedipus killed the Sphinx. Find three other such riddles and create a quiz board to test your friends on the riddles.

❏ Use a Venn diagram to compare and contrast Greek plays with modern-day plays.

❏ Free choice: Submit a proposal form for a product of your choice.

80 points

❏ Create an informational video that uses *Oedipus Rex* to explain the components of a Greek tragedy. Be sure and include at least three quotes in your video!

❏ Design social media profiles for Oedipus and his mother. Have them post statuses and interact as they consider the prophecy and death of Laius.

Name: _____

Oedipus Rex

Directions: Choose at least two activities from the options below. The activities must total 100 points. Place a checkmark next to each box to show which activities you will complete. All activities must be completed by: _____.

---

20 points

❏ Tragic heroes have both admirable traits and a flaw. Make a T-chart that identifies these characteristics in Oedipus.

❏ Use a Venn diagram to compare and contrast the format and organization of Greek plays with modern-day plays.

---

50 points

❏ Is Oedipus a good example of a tragic hero? Create a three-dimensional time-line that proves your opinion through events and quotes.

❏ Prepare a poster that shares the importance of the Chorus not only in this play, but Greek plays in general.

❏ By answering the Riddle of the Sphinx, Oedipus killed the Sphinx. Brainstorm at least six other such riddles and create a quiz board to test your friends on the riddles.

❏ Design social media profiles for Oedipus and his mother. Have them post statuses and interact as they consider the prophecy and death of Laius.

---

80 points

❏ Perform a modern-day play of *Oedipus Rex*. Use the same names for each character but update the language and plot. Use at least two quotes from the original play in your remake.

❏ Free choice: Submit a proposal form for a product of your choice.

Oedipus Rex

Directions: Choose at least two activities from the options below. The activities must total 100 points. Place a checkmark next to each box to show which activities you will complete. All activities must be completed by: _____.

20 points

- ☐ By answering the Riddle of the Sphinx, Oedipus killed the Sphinx. Brainstorm other such riddles and create a quiz board to test your friends on the riddles.
- ☐ Use a Venn diagram to compare and contrast various aspects of Greek plays with modern-day plays.

50 points

- ☐ Create an informational video that uses *Oedipus Rex* to explain the components of a Greek tragedy. Be sure and include at least five quotes in your video!
- ☐ Is Oedipus a good example of a tragic hero? Create a three-dimensional time-line that proves your opinion through events and quotes.
- ☐ Design social media profiles for Oedipus and his mother. Have them post statuses and interact as they consider the prophecy and death of Laius.
- ☐ Free choice: Submit a proposal form for a product of your choice.

80 points

- ☐ Perform a modern-day play of *Oedipus Rex*. Use the same names for each character but update the language and plot. Use at least two quotes from the original play in your remake.
- ☐ Select a tragic hero from history. Conduct an interview in which you speak with Oedipus and the hero you selected to compare and contrast their lives.

Macbeth

List Menu

Reading Objectives Covered Through These Menus and These Activities

- Students will represent textual evidence and use it to prove conclusions.
- Students will make and explain inferences made from the story.
- Students will analyze the various literary aspects of a story.
- Students will represent textual evidence by using story maps.
- Students will analyze characters, their relationships, and their importance in the story.
- Students will recognize and analyze story plot and problem resolution.

Writing Objectives Covered Through These Menus and These Activities

- Students will write to express their feelings, inform, explain, describe, narrate, entertain, persuade, reflect, or problem solve.
- Students will support their responses with textual evidence.

Materials Needed by Students for Completion

- *Macbeth* by William Shakespeare
- Poster board or large white paper
- Map of Scotland ▲ ●
- Magazines (for collages)
- Recycled materials (for models ●, dioramas)
- Graph paper or Internet access (for crossword puzzles) ▲
- Story map ▲
- Materials for board games (folders, colored cards, etc.) ▲
- Microsoft PowerPoint or other slideshow software ● ■
- DVD or VHS recorder (for videos)
- Internet access (for WebQuests) ■

Special Notes on the Modifications of These Menus

- Because a List menu is a point-based menu, it is easy to provide additional modifications by simply changing the point goal for those students who need it. The bottom of the menu has a short contract that can be used to record any changes. The two-page format of the triangle ▲ and circle ● menus also allow for additional modification by mixing and matching the pages. The front of each of these two-page menus has the lower and middle-level activities, while the second page has the higher level activities and contract. Additional modifications can be made by using the first page from the circle menu ● with the second page from the triangle menu ▲. This will allow students a little more flexibility when approaching the higher level activities.

Special Notes on the Use of These Menus

- These menus give students the opportunity to create a video. Although students enjoy producing their own videos, there often are difficulties obtaining the equipment and scheduling the use of a video recorder. This activity can be modified by allowing students to act out the product (like a play) or, if students have the technology, allowing them to produce a webcam version of their presentation.
- These menus ask students to use recycled materials to create their dioramas and models ●. This does not mean only plastic and paper; instead, students should focus on using materials in new ways. It works well if a box is started for "recycled" contributions at the beginning of the school year. That way, students always have access to these types of materials.
- The square menu ■ allows students to create a WebQuest. There are multiple versions and templates for WebQuests available on the Internet. Teachers should decide whether to specify a certain format or allow students to create one of their own choosing.

Time Frame

- 1–2 weeks—Students are given the menu as the unit is started, and the guidelines and point expectations are discussed. Students usually will need to earn 100 points for 100%, although there is an opportunity for extra credit if the teacher would like to use another target number. Because this menu covers one topic in depth, the teacher will go over all of the options for the topic being covered and have students place check marks in the boxes next to the activities they are most interested in completing. Teachers will need to set aside a few moments to sign the agreement at the bottom of the page with each student. As instruction continues, activities are completed by students and submitted to the teacher for grading.
- 1–2 days—The teacher chooses an activity or product from an objective to use with the entire class during that lesson time.

Suggested Forms

- All-purpose rubric
- Student presentation rubric
- Proposal form for point-based products

Macbeth: Side 1

Guidelines:

1. You may complete as many of the activities listed within the time period.
2. You may choose any combination of activities.
3. Your goal is 100 points. You may earn up to _____ points extra credit.
4. You may be as creative as you like within the guidelines listed below.
5. You must show your plan to your teacher by _____.
6. Activities may be turned in at any time during the working time period. They will be graded and recorded on this sheet as you continue to work, so keep it safe!

Plan to Do	Activity to Complete (Side 1: 15–20 points)	Point Value	Date Completed	Points Earned
	Make a collage of words and pictures that describe an ideal king. Use your collage to write a paragraph about qualities an effective king should possess.	15		
	Create a poster that shows the inside of the Globe Theatre.	15		
	Using a map of Scotland, indicate the locations mentioned in this play.	15		
	Change 15 lines of the play into a song or rap and perform it for your classmates.	20		
	Create a crossword puzzle about the characters and events in *Macbeth*.	20		
	Create a picture dictionary for at least 10 words Shakespeare uses in *Macbeth* that are no longer used today.	20		
	Design a diorama that could be used as a set for this play.	20		
	Complete a story map for *Macbeth*.	20		
	Total number of points you are planning to earn from Side 1.	**Total points earned from Side 1:**		

Macbeth: Side 2

Guidelines:

1. You may complete as many of the activities listed within the time period.
2. You may choose any combination of activities.
3. Your goal is 100 points. You may earn up to _____ points extra credit.
4. You may be as creative as you like within the guidelines listed below.
5. You must show your plan to your teacher by _____.
6. Activities may be turned in at any time during the working time period. They will be graded and recorded on this sheet as you continue to work, so keep it safe!

Plan to Do	Activity to Complete (Side 2: 25–35 points)	Point Value	Date Completed	Points Earned
	Make a board game for this play using the characters and plot as the theme for your game.	25		
	Write an obituary for one of the characters who dies at the end of the play.	25		
	Select a scene from *Macbeth* and rewrite it in modern-day language. *Note*: This "translation" must be your own and not taken from another source.	30		
	Come to school as one of the characters from *Macbeth* and tell us about yourself.	30		
	Create a video that could be used as a movie trailer for *Macbeth*.	30		
	Turn *Macbeth* into a modern-day classic by recording a video of the play using modern terms and themes.	35		
	Write a one-act play that focuses on the next prophecy of the three witches.	35		
	Free choice: Submit your free choice proposal form for a product of your choice.			
	Total number of points you are planning to earn from Side 1.	**Total points earned from Side 1:**		
	Total number of points you are planning to earn from Side 2.	**Total points earned from Side 2:**		
		Grand Total (/100)		

I am planning to complete _____ activities that could earn up to a total of _____ points.

Teacher's initials _____ Student's signature _____

Macbeth: Side 1

Guidelines:

1. You may complete as many of the activities listed within the time period.
2. You may choose any combination of activities.
3. Your goal is 100 points. You may earn up to _____ points extra credit.
4. You may be as creative as you like within the guidelines listed below.
5. You must show your plan to your teacher by _____.
6. Activities may be turned in at any time during the working time period. They will be graded and recorded on this sheet as you continue to work, so keep it safe!

Plan to Do	Activity to Complete (Side 1: 10–20 points)	Point Value	Date Completed	Points Earned
	Using a map of Scotland, indicate the locations mentioned in this play. Use a key that is meaningful to the play to show each location.	10		
	Change 25 lines of the play into a song or rap and perform it for your classmates.	15		
	Create a picture dictionary for at least 15 words Shakespeare uses in *Macbeth* that are no longer used today.	15		
	Make a collage of words and pictures that describe an ideal king. Use your collage to write a paragraph about qualities an effective king should possess.	15		
	Construct a cross section model of the Globe Theatre.	20		
	Design a diorama that could be used as a set for *Macbeth*.	20		
	Record a speech that Malcolm could have given to the people to reassure them when he takes the throne.	20		
	Write an obituary for one of the characters who dies in Macbeth.	20		
	Total number of points you are planning to earn from Side 1.	**Total points earned from Side 1:**		

Name: _____

Macbeth: Side 2

Guidelines:

1. You may complete as many of the activities listed within the time period.
2. You may choose any combination of activities.
3. Your goal is 100 points. You may earn up to _____ points extra credit.
4. You may be as creative as you like within the guidelines listed below.
5. You must show your plan to your teacher by _____.
6. Activities may be turned in at any time during the working time period. They will be graded and recorded on this sheet as you continue to work, so keep it safe!

Plan to Do	Activity to Complete (Side 2: 25–30 points)	Point Value	Date Completed	Points Earned
	Select a scene from *Macbeth* and rewrite it in modern-day language. *Note*: This "translation" must be your own and not taken from another source.	25		
	Come to school as one of the characters from *Macbeth* and discuss your impact on the play's events.	25		
	Create a video that could be used as a movie trailer for *Macbeth*.	25		
	Write a newspaper article that covers the event that takes place between Macbeth and Duncan.	25		
	Create a PowerPoint presentation in which you analyze one of Macbeth's character traits. Include quotes, pictures, and evidence of the trait you have selected.	30		
	Turn *Macbeth* into a modern-day classic by recording a video of the play using modern terms and themes.	30		
	Write a one-act play that focuses on the next prophecy of the three witches.	30		
	Free choice: Submit your free choice proposal form for a product of your choice.			
	Total number of points you are planning to earn from Side 1.	**Total points earned from Side 1:**		
	Total number of points you are planning to earn from Side 2.	**Total points earned from Side 2:**		
		Grand Total (/100)		

I am planning to complete _____ activities that could earn up to a total of _____ points.

Teacher's initials _____ Student's signature _____

Name: _____ ■

Macbeth

Guidelines:

1. You may complete as many of the activities listed within the time period.
2. You may choose any combination of activities.
3. Your goal is 100 points. You may earn up to _____ points extra credit.
4. You may be as creative as you like within the guidelines listed below.
5. You must show your plan to your teacher by _____.
6. Activities may be turned in at any time during the working time period. They will be graded and recorded on this sheet as you continue to work, so keep it safe!

Plan to Do	Activity to Complete	Point Value	Date Completed	Points Earned
	Make a collage of words and pictures that describe an ideal king. Use your collage to write a paragraph about qualities an effective king should possess.	10		
	Create a picture dictionary for at least 20 words Shakespeare uses that are no longer used today.	15		
	Design a diorama that shows the prophecy of the three witches coming true.	15		
	Create a video that could be used as a movie trailer for *Macbeth*.	20		
	Design a WebQuest that allows questors to learn more about Shakespeare, his works, and the Globe Theatre.	20		
	Record a speech that Malcolm could have given to the people to reassure them when he takes the throne.	20		
	Select a scene from *Macbeth* and rewrite it in modern-day language. *Note*: This "translation" must be your own and not taken from another source.	20		
	Write an obituary for one of the characters who dies at the end of the play.	20		
	Come to school as one of the characters from *Macbeth* and discuss your strengths and weaknesses as a character.	25		
	Create a PowerPoint presentation with historical and real-world examples that mirror Macbeth's actions regarding the desire for power.	25		
	Turn *Macbeth* into a modern-day classic by recording a video of the play using modern terms and themes.	25		
	Who is guiltier, Lady Macbeth or Macbeth? Determine a defendable thesis statement and write an essay that answers this question using quotes and evidence from the play.	25		
	Write a one-act play that focuses on the next prophecy of the three witches.	25		
	Free choice: Submit your free choice proposal form for a product of your choice.			
	Total number of points you are planning to earn.		**Total points earned:**	

I am planning to complete _____ activities that could earn up to a total of _____ points.

Teacher's initials _____ Student's signature _____

The Canterbury Tales

20-50-80 Menu

Reading Objectives Covered Through These Menus and These Activities

- Students will represent textual evidence and use it to prove conclusions.
- Students will compare one literary work with another.
- Students will make and explain inferences made from the story.
- Students will analyze the various literary aspects of a story.
- Students will analyze characters, their relationships, and their importance in the story.
- Students will recognize and analyze story plot and problem resolution.

Writing Objectives Covered Through These Menus and These Activities

- Students will write to express their feelings, inform, explain, describe, narrate, entertain, persuade, reflect, or problem solve.
- Students will exhibit voice in their writing.
- Students will use vivid language.

Materials Needed by Students for Completion

- *The Canterbury Tales* by Geoffrey Chaucer
- Poster board or large white paper
- Materials for board games (folders, colored cards, etc.) ▲
- Coat hangers (for mobiles) ▲
- String (for mobiles) ▲
- Blank index cards (for mobiles ▲, trading cards)
- DVD or VHS recorder (for commercials ▲ ●, documentaries ■)
- Options for electronic presentations (Microsoft PowerPoint, Prezi, Slideshare, Animoto, etc.) ■
- Aluminum foil (for quiz boards) ● ■
- Holiday lights (for quiz boards) ● ■
- Wires (for quiz boards) ● ■

Special Notes on the Modifications of These Menus

- If needed, further modifications can be made to a 20-50-80 menu based on the needs of your students. The easiest modification is altering the point goal from 100; lowering or raising the goal on a menu by 10 (or 20) points is appropriate if additional modification up or down is needed.

Special Notes on the Use of These Menus

- These menus give students the opportunity to create a commercial ▲ ● and documentary ■. Although students enjoy producing their own videos, there often are difficulties obtaining the equipment and scheduling the use of a video recorder. This activity can be modified by allowing students to act out the product (like a play) or, if students have the technology, allowing them to produce a webcam versionof their presentation.
- The circle ● and square ■ menus provide the opportunity for students to create a quiz board. A student friendly informational sheet that offers the steps for constructing their own quiz board is available at http://www.cesi-science.org/attachments/article/100/QuizBoardDirections.pdf.

Time Frame

- 1–2 weeks—Students are given a menu as the unit is started, and the teacher discusses all of the product options on the menu. As the different options are discussed, students will choose the activities they are most interested in completing so they meet their goal of 100 points. As the lessons progress through the week(s), the teacher and students refer back to the menu options associated with the content being taught.
- 1–2 days—The teacher chooses an activity or product from the menu to use with the entire class.

Suggested Forms

- All-purpose rubric
- Student presentation rubric
- Proposal form for point-based projects

Name: _____ ▲

The Canterbury Tales

Directions: Choose at least two activities from the options below. The activities must total 100 points. Place a checkmark next to each box to show which activities you will complete. All activities must be completed by: _____.

---

20 points

☐ Create a set of trading cards for the different characters we have experienced. Include at least one quote on each card that describes that character.

☐ Make a mobile that shows how the different pilgrims are grouped by class.

---

50 points

☐ Create a children's book in which you illustrate your favorite Canterbury Tale.

☐ Design a board game that asks questions and shares the adventures found in *The Canterbury Tales*.

☐ Write a three facts and a fib about one of the characters in a tale we have read.

☐ Free choice: Submit a proposal form for a product of your choice.

---

80 points

☐ Design a social media page for two of the pilgrims from *The Canterbury Tales* you have read about. These two pilgrims should comment on each other's social media page.

☐ Read at least two additional tales that you have not been assigned. Create a commercial to entice your classmates to read these two Canterbury Tales as well.

Name: _____

The Canterbury Tales

Directions: Choose at least two activities from the options below. The activities must total 100 points. Place a checkmark next to each box to show which activities you will complete. All activities must be completed by: _____.

20 points

❏ Create a set of trading cards for the different characters we have experienced. Include at least one quote on each card that describes that character.

❏ Make a mind map that shows how the different pilgrims are grouped by class.

50 points

❏ Create a quiz board to quiz your classmates on the events in different pilgrims' tales.

❏ Design a social media page for two of the pilgrims from *The Canterbury Tales* you have read about. These two pilgrims should comment on each other's social media page.

❏ Based on the traits they exhibit, create a windowpane in which you match the different pilgrims with a well-known celebrity or historical figure.

❏ Free choice: Submit a proposal form for a product of your choice.

80 points

❏ Write your own modern-day Canterbury Tale using a modern pilgrim with a present-day purpose, but using Chaucer's writing style.

❏ Read at least two additional tales that you have not been assigned. Create a commercial to entice your classmates to read these two Canterbury Tales as well.

The Canterbury Tales

Directions: Choose at least two activities from the options below. The activities must total 100 points. Place a checkmark next to each box to show which activities you will complete. All activities must be completed by: _____.

20 points

☐ Create a set of trading cards for the different characters we have experienced. Include at least one quote on each card that describes that character.

☐ Create a quiz board to quiz your classmates on the events in different pilgrims' tales.

50 points

☐ Design a social media page for two of the pilgrims from *The Canterbury Tales* you have read about. These two pilgrims should comment on each other's social media page.

☐ Read at least two additional tales that you have not been assigned. Create a commercial to entice your classmates to read these two Canterbury Tales as well.

☐ Write a three facts and a fib about one of the characters in a tale we have read.

☐ Free choice: Submit a proposal form for a *The Canterbury Tales* product of your choice.

80 points

☐ Write your own modern-day Canterbury tale using a modern pilgrim with a present-day purpose, but using Chaucer's writing style.

☐ Record a documentary (or create an electronic presentation) in which you analyze the different stereotypes found in *The Canterbury Tales*.

The Scarlet Letter

Meal Menu ▲ and Tic-Tac-Toe Menu ● ■

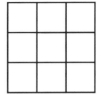

Reading Objectives Covered Through These Menus and These Activities

- Students will represent textual evidence and use it to prove conclusions.
- Students will make and explain inferences made from the story.
- Students will analyze the various literary aspects of a story.
- Students will analyze characters, their relationships, and their importance in the story.
- Students will recognize and analyze story plot and problem resolution.

Writing Objectives Covered Through These Menus and These Activities

- Students will write to express their feelings, inform, explain, describe, narrate, entertain, develop, influence, persuade, reflect, or problem solve.
- Students will support their responses with textual evidence.

Materials Needed by Students for Completion

- *The Scarlet Letter* by Nathaniel Hawthorne
- Poster board or large white paper
- DVD or VHS recorder (for videos)
- Magazines (for collages)
- Coat hangers (for mobiles) ▲
- String (for mobiles) ▲
- Blank index cards (for mobiles) ▲
- Recycled materials (for models) ▲
- Microsoft PowerPoint or other slideshow software ■

Special Notes on the Modifications of These Menus

- This topic has two different menu formats: The Meal menu (▲) and Tic-Tac-Toe (● ■) menu. The Meal menu is specifically selected for the triangle ▲ option as it easily allows the menu to be broken into manageable bits; the different meals separate the page, making it less daunting for special needs students. The space between the meals makes it easy for the teacher to cut the menu as needed based on the comfort level of the students. If it is the first time choice is being introduced, then the children may receive only the strip of the top breakfast options. Then, when they have finished one of those options, they can receive a strip of lunches and finally, the enrichment-level dinner and dessert activities. After students have grown more accustomed to making choices, the menu might be cut just once after the lunch options, so students can select a breakfast and a lunch and submit them to the teacher. Then, they can choose from the dinner strip they receive. The ultimate goal would be for students to have all nine options at once and not be overwhelmed.

Special Notes on the Use of These Menus

- These menus give students the opportunity to create a video. Although students enjoy producing their own videos, there often are difficulties obtaining the equipment and scheduling the use of a video recorder. This activity can be modified by allowing students to act out the product (like a play) or, if students have the technology, allowing them to produce a webcam version of their presentation.
- The triangle menu ▲ asks students to use recycled materials to create their model. This does not mean only plastic and paper; instead, students should focus on using materials in new ways. It works well if a box is started for "recycled" contributions at the beginning of the school year. That way, students always have access to these types of materials.

Time Frame

- 2–3 weeks—Students are given the menu as the unit is started. As the teacher presents lessons throughout the week, he or she should refer back to the menu options associated with that content. The teacher will go over all of the options for that content and have students place check marks in the boxes that represent the activities they are most interested in completing. As students choose activities, they should complete a column or a row. When students complete this pattern, they have completed one activity from each content area, learning style, or level of Bloom's revised taxonomy, depending on the design of the menu.
- 1 week—At the start of the unit, the teacher chooses the three activities he or she feels are most valuable for students. Stations can be set up in the classroom. These three activities are available for student choice throughout the week as regular instruction takes place.
- 1–2 days—The teacher chooses an activity from the menu to use with the entire class.

Suggested Forms

- All-purpose rubric
- Student presentation rubric
- Student-taught lesson rubric ● ■
- Free-choice proposal form

The Scarlet Letter

Directions: Choose one activity each for breakfast, lunch, and dinner. Dessert is an activity you can choose to do after you have finished your other meals. All products must be completed by: _____.

Breakfast

❑ Create a brochure that explains the rules and expectations for those who live in a Puritan society.

❑ Use a Venn diagram to compare the Puritan society to our society.

❑ Record a video that shares information about the Puritan beliefs.

Lunch

❑ Prepare a character poster in which you show quotes and information about Hester.

❑ Create a collage of five quotes that share information about Hester and her values. Include a brief explanation for each quote.

❑ Design a Hester and Me mobile in which you compare your beliefs to Hester's beliefs.

Dinner

❑ Write a newspaper article that covers the story of Hester and Pearl.

❑ Reenact the scene on the scaffold in Chapter 23.

❑ Free choice: Submit a free choice proposal about the events in *The Scarlet Letter* to your teacher for approval.

Dessert

❑ Select at least three famous people who you feel the Puritans would punish with a letter other than an A. Make a poster of the people and the letter each would be assigned.

❑ Create a model of the book as it is described in the introduction to the story.

The Scarlet Letter

Directions: Check the boxes you plan to complete. They should form a tic-tac-toe across or down. All products are due by: _____.

☐ Hester	☐ Society's Rules	☐ Dimmesdale
Create a collage of quotes that share information about Hester and her values. Include a brief explanation for each quote that provides insight into Hester's personality.	Record a video that shares information about the Puritan beliefs. During your video, compare this society with a strict religious society found in present day.	During the story, Dimmesdale falls ill. Think about the circumstances surrounding his illness and write another ending to *The Scarlet Letter* that could have led to his going to Europe.
☐ Give Me an A!	☐ **Free Choice:** *On Hester's Character* (Fill out your proposal form before beginning the free choice!)	☐ A Reenactment
Select at least five historical figures who you feel the Puritans would punish with a letter other than an A. Make a poster of the people and the letter each would be assigned. Include a short paragraph for each explaining his or her deeds and your letter choice.		Reenact the scene where Hester fights to keep Pearl. Use at least three quotes in your reenactment of this scene.
☐ Symbolism	☐ Lessons Learned	☐ Hester
Prepare a student-taught lesson on the use of Pearl as a symbol in *The Scarlet Letter*. Use quotes to support your observations.	Write a newspaper article that covers the story of Hester, Dimmesdale, and Chillingworth.	Prepare a character trait poster in which you show how Hester changes and develops as the story progresses. Include a quote that shows each change.

The Scarlet Letter

Directions: Check the boxes you plan to complete. They should form a tic-tac-toe across or down. All products are due by: _____.

☐ Hester	☐ Society's Rules	☐ Dimmesdale
Create a collage of quotes that show how Pearl views her mother. Include a brief explanation for each quote that provides insight into Hester and Pearl's relationship.	How much has society changed since Hester's time? Record a video in which you share various ways that your high school life is similar to what Hester may have experienced during Puritan times.	During the story, Dimmesdale falls ill. Think about the circumstances surrounding his illness and write another ending to *The Scarlet Letter* in which his illness is addressed in a different way.
☐ Give Me an A!	☐ **Free Choice: On Hester's Character** (Fill out your proposal form before beginning the free choice!)	☐ A Reenactment
Select at least 10 historical figures who you feel the Puritans would punish with a letter other than an A. Make a poster of the people and the letter each would be assigned. Include a short paragraph for each explaining his or her deeds and your letter choice.		Reenact the most important scene in *The Scarlet Letter*. Use at least five direct quotes in your reenactment.
☐ Symbolism	☐ Lessons Learned	☐ Hester
Prepare a student-taught lesson on the symbols found in *The Scarlet Letter*. Although you can mention the letter A, try and focus on the other symbols found in the novel. Use quotes to support your observations.	Create a PowerPoint presentation in which you use quotes from *The Scarlet Letter* to share at least four lessons that can apply to your daily life.	Write a newspaper article that explains how Hester could be considered one of the first literary feminists. Include at least three quotes to support your opinions.

The Great Gatsby

Three-Topic List Menu

Reading Objectives Covered Through These Menus and These Activities

- Students will represent textual evidence and use it to prove conclusions.
- Students will make and explain inferences made from the story.
- Students will analyze the various literary aspects of a story.
- Students will represent textual evidence by using story maps.
- Students will compare different forms of a written work (written versus performed).
- Students will analyze characters, their relationships, and their importance in the story.
- Students will recognize and analyze story plot and problem resolution.

Writing Objectives Covered Through These Menus and These Activities

- Students will write to express their feelings, inform, explain, describe, narrate, entertain, persuade, reflect, or problem solve.
- Students will support their responses with textual evidence.
- Students will exhibit voice in their writing.

Materials Needed by Students for Completion

- *The Great Gatsby* by F. Scott Fitzgerald
- Poster board or large white paper
- Materials for board games (folders, colored cards, etc.) ●
- Coat hangers (for mobiles) ▲
- String (for mobiles) ▲
- Blank index cards (for mobiles) ▲
- DVD or VHS recorder (for videos ▲   ●, news reports)
- Story map
- Microsoft PowerPoint or other slideshow software
- Recycled materials (for dioramas) ▲
- Scrapbooking materials ■

Special Notes on the Modifications of These Menus

- Because a List menu is a point-based menu, it is easy to provide additional modifications by simply changing the point goal for those students who need it. The bottom of the menu has a short contract that can be used to record any changes.

Novels, Short Stories, and Drama

Special Notes on the Use of These Menus

- These menus give students the opportunity to create a video ▲ ● or news report. Although students enjoy producing their own videos, there often are difficulties obtaining the equipment and scheduling the use of a video recorder. This activity can be modified by allowing students to act out the product (like a play) or, if students have the technology, allowing them to produce a webcam version of their presentation.
- These menus allow students to create a bulletin board display. Some classrooms may only have one bulletin board, so the teacher can divide the board into sections, or additional classroom wall or hall space can be sectioned off for the creation of these displays. Students can plan their display based on the amount of space they are assigned.
- The triangle menu ▲ asks students to use recycled materials to create their dioramas. This does not mean only plastic and paper; instead, students should focus on using materials in new ways. It works well if a box is started for "recycled" contributions at the beginning of the school year. That way, students always have access to these types of materials.

Time Frame

- 1–2 weeks—Students are given the menu as the unit is started, and the guidelines and point expectations are discussed. Students usually will need to earn 100 points for 100%, although there is an opportunity for extra credit if the teacher would like to use another target number. Because this menu covers three topics in depth, the teacher may choose to only go over the options for the topic being covered first; the students place check marks in the boxes next to the activities they are most interested in completing. As instruction continues, additional explanation of the new topic activities can be provided. Once students have access to the entire menu, teachers will need to set aside a few moments to sign the agreement at the bottom of the page with each student. As activities are completed by students, they will be submitted to the teacher for grading.
- 1–2 days—The teacher chooses an activity or product from an objective to use with the entire class during that lesson time.

Suggested Forms

- All-purpose rubric
- Student presentation rubric
- Proposal form for point-based products

129

Name: _____ ▲

The Great Gatsby: Side 1

Guidelines:

1. You may complete as many of the activities listed as you can within the time period.
2. You may choose any combination of activities, but **must** complete at least one activity from each topic area.
3. Your goal is 100 points. You may earn up to _____ points extra credit.
4. You may be as creative as you like within the guidelines listed below.
5. You must share your plan with your teacher by _____.
6. Activities may be turned in at any time during the working time period. They will be graded and recorded on this sheet as you continue to work, so keep it safe!

Topic	Plan to Do	Activity to Complete	Point Value	Date Completed	Points Earned
Setting		Draw a mural that shows the valley of ashes.	15		
		Make a diorama to show the difference between the valley of ashes and West Egg.	20		
		Design a windowpane that shows West Egg, East Egg, the valley of ashes, and New York City. Record one quote that describes each location.	25		
		Write and perform a song about someone who lives in West Egg.	30		
Characters		Make a mobile that shows information about all of the characters. Include a drawing of each.	15		
		Create a three facts and a fib about one of the characters in *The Great Gatsby*.	20		
		Which character is most like you? Create a Venn diagram to compare and contrast yourself with one of the characters.	25		
		Record an interview in which you pretend to interview one of the characters from *The Great Gatsby* about his or her life.	30		
		Total number of points you are planning to earn from Side 1.	**Total points earned from Side 1:**		

Name: _____   ▲

The Great Gatsby: Side 2

Guidelines:

1. You may complete as many of the activities listed as you can within the time period.
2. You may choose any combination of activities, but **must** complete at least one activity from each topic area.
3. Your goal is 100 points. You may earn up to _____ points extra credit.
4. You may be as creative as you like within the guidelines listed below.
5. You must share your plan with your teacher by _____.
6. Activities may be turned in at any time during the working time period. They will be graded and recorded on this sheet as you continue to work, so keep it safe!

Topic	Plan to Do	Activity to Complete	Point Value	Date Completed	Points Earned
Plot		Complete a story map for *The Great Gatsby*.	15		
		Create a worksheet of questions that focuses on how the plot develops. Do not forget to include an answer key!	20		
		Record a news report in which you discuss the events that take place in Chapter 8.	25		
		Write a children's book about how Gatsby came to live in East Egg.	30		
Analysis		Make an advertisement to convince others to read *The Great Gatsby*. Include why it is worth reading.	15		
		Create a PowerPoint presentation with at least five quotes from *The Great Gatsby* that would be relevant advice for someone today.	20		
		In *The Great Gatsby*, wealth could determine a person's social class. Create a bulletin board display that shows how this happened in the story.	25		
		Record a video that compares the written version of *The Great Gatsby* with any of the motion picture versions.	30		
Any		**Free choice:** Submit your free choice proposal form for a product of your choice.			
		Total number of points you are planning to earn from Side 1.	**Total points earned from Side 1:**		
		Total number of points you are planning to earn from Side 2.	**Total points earned from Side 2:**		
			Grand Total (/100)		

I am planning to complete _____ activities that could earn up to a total of _____ points.

Teacher's initials _____ Student's signature _____

Name: _____   ●

The Great Gatsby: Side 1

Guidelines:

1. You may complete as many of the activities listed as you can within the time period.
2. You may choose any combination of activities, but **must** complete at least one activity from each topic area.
3. Your goal is 100 points. You may earn up to _____ points extra credit.
4. You may be as creative as you like within the guidelines listed below.
5. You must share your plan with your teacher by _____.
6. Activities may be turned in at any time during the working time period. They will be graded and recorded on this sheet as you continue to work, so keep it safe!

Topic	Plan to Do	Activity to Complete	Point Value	Date Completed	Points Earned
Setting		Draw a mural that shows the valley of ashes. Include at least three quotes around the mural to describe it.	15		
		Design a windowpane that shows West Egg, East Egg, the valley of ashes, and New York City. Record at least one quote that describes each location.	20		
		Design a bumper sticker that could be used to describe one of the four areas discussed in *The Great Gatsby*.	25		
		Write a children's book about a child who grows up in the valley of ashes and ends up living in East Egg.	30		
Characters		Create a three facts and a fib about one of the characters in *The Great Gatsby*.	15		
		Make a Venn diagram to compare how we view Gatsby at the beginning of the novel and at the end of the novel. (Use at least two quotes for each view.)	20		
		Make a board game in which players go through the game as characters in the novel and respond to choices as their character would.	25		
		Pretend that you are interviewing Gatsby on his childhood. After brainstorming the interview questions, provide his answers using quotes from the novel.	30		
		Total number of points you are planning to earn from Side 1.		**Total points earned from Side 1:**	

The Great Gatsby: Side 2

Guidelines:

1. You may complete as many of the activities listed as you can within the time period.
2. You may choose any combination of activities, but **must** complete at least one activity from each topic area.
3. Your goal is 100 points. You may earn up to _____ points extra credit.
4. You may be as creative as you like within the guidelines listed below.
5. You must share your plan with your teacher by _____.
6. Activities may be turned in at any time during the working time period. They will be graded and recorded on this sheet as you continue to work, so keep it safe!

Topic	Plan to Do	Activity to Complete	Point Value	Date Completed	Points Earned
Plot		Complete a story map for *The Great Gatsby*.	15		
		Record a news report in which you discuss the events that take place in Chapter 8.	20		
		Create a worksheet of questions that focuses on how the plot develops. Do not forget to include an answer key!	25		
		Rewrite a chapter of the book that contains an event you would have liked to have gone differently.	30		
Analysis		Create a PowerPoint presentation with at least eight quotes from *The Great Gatsby* that would be relevant advice for someone today.	15		
		In *The Great Gatsby*, wealth could determine a person's social class. Create a bulletin board display that shows how this was possible in Gatsby's time.	20		
		Record a video that compares the written version of *The Great Gatsby* with one of the motion picture versions.	25		
		Write an essay that shares how the American Dream is still being pursued in today's society.	30		
Any		**Free choice:** Submit your free choice proposal form for a product of your choice.			
		Total number of points you are planning to earn from Side 1.	**Total points earned from Side 1:**		
		Total number of points you are planning to earn from Side 2.	**Total points earned from Side 2:**		
			Grand Total (/100)		

I am planning to complete _____ activities that could earn up to a total of _____ points.

Teacher's initials _____ Student's signature _____

Name: _____

The Great Gatsby

Guidelines:

1. You may complete as many of the activities listed as you can within the time period.
2. You may choose any combination of activities, but **must** complete at least one activity from each topic area.
3. Your goal is 100 points. You may earn up to _____ points extra credit.
4. You may be as creative as you like within the guidelines listed below.
5. You must share your plan with your teacher by _____.
6. Activities may be turned in at any time during the working time period. They will be graded and recorded on this sheet as you continue to work, so keep it safe!

Topic	Plan to Do	Activity to Complete	Point Value	Date Completed	Points Earned
Setting		Draw a mural that shows the valley of ashes. Include at least three quotes around the mural to describe it.	10		
		Design a windowpane that shows the important setting locations in *The Great Gatsby*. Record a quote that describes each location.	15		
		Prepare a speech that shares how weather accentuates the plot and emotions throughout the story. Be sure and include quotes to support your examples.	20		
		It is said that each geographical area symbolizes a character found in this novel. Create a scrapbook that shares quotes describing each area, and the character who you feel is its match.	25		
Characters		Create a three facts and a fib about one of the minor characters in *The Great Gatsby*.	10		
		Gatsby has worked very hard to reinvent himself. Make a mind map that provides examples of the ways he has changed from childhood through the end of the novel.	15		
		Make a Venn diagram to compare how Gatsby views Daisy and her true character. (Use at least two quotes for each view.)	20		
		Pretend that you are interviewing Gatsby on his childhood. After brainstorming the interview questions, provide his answers using quotes from the novel.	25		
Plot		Complete a story map for *The Great Gatsby*.	10		
		Record a news report in which you discuss the events that lead up to (and including) the event in Chapter 8.	15		
		Make a poster that shows how the different characters change with each major event in the story. Include quotes to support the changes you note.	20		
		The Great Gatsby is filled with "what ifs" that could drastically change the outcome of the novel. Select one of these events and use it to rewrite the book from that point forward.	25		
Analysis		Create a PowerPoint presentation with at least 10 quotes from *The Great Gatsby* that could still be relevant advice for someone in today's society.	10		
		In *The Great Gatsby*, wealth could determine a person's social class. Create a bulletin board display that shows if this is still true in today's society.	15		
		Write a newspaper article that reviews the written version of *The Great Gatsby* with any of the motion picture versions. Include an in-depth critique in your comparison of the two works.	20		
		Write an essay that documents the role the American Dream takes throughout the themes and plot of *The Great Gatsby*.	25		
Any		Free choice: Submit your free choice proposal form for a product of your choice.			
		Total number of points you are planning to earn.		**Total points earned:**	

I am planning to complete _____ activities that could earn up to a total of _____ points.

Teacher's initials _____ Student's signature _____

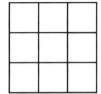

A Farewell to Arms

Meal Menu ▲ and
Tic-Tac-Toe Menu ● ■

Reading Objectives Covered Through These Menus and These Activities

- Students will represent textual evidence and use it to prove conclusions.
- Students will make and explain inferences made from the story.
- Students will analyze the various literary aspects of a story.
- Students will represent textual evidence by using story maps.
- Students will analyze characters, their relationships, and their importance in the story.
- Students will recognize and analyze story plot and problem resolution.

Writing Objectives Covered Through These Menus and These Activities

- Students will write to express their feelings, inform, explain, describe, narrate, entertain, develop, influence, persuade, reflect, or problem solve.
- Students will support their responses with textual evidence.

Materials Needed by Students for Completion

- *A Farewell to Arms* by Ernest Hemingway
- Poster board or large white paper
- Blank index cards (for trading cards) ▲
- Story map ▲
- Recycled materials (for dioramas) ▲
- DVD or VHS recorder (for commercials, news reports ● ■)
- Graph paper or Internet access (for crossword puzzles) ▲
- Microsoft PowerPoint or other slideshow software ●
- Scrapbooking materials ● ■

Special Notes on the Modifications of These Menus

- This topic has two different menu formats: The Meal menu ▲ and Tic-Tac-Toe ● ■ menu. The Meal menu is specifically selected for the triangle ▲ option as it easily allows the menu to be broken into manageable bits; the different meals separate the page, making it less daunting for special needs students. The space between the meals makes it easy for the teacher to cut the menu as needed based on the comfort level of the students. If it is the first time choice is being introduced, then the children may receive only the strip of the top breakfast options. Then, when they have finished one of those options, they can receive a strip of lunches and finally, the enrichment-level dinner and dessert activities. After students have grown more accustomed to making choices, the menu might be cut just once after the lunch options, so students can select a breakfast and a lunch and submit them to the teacher. Then, they can choose from the dinner strip they receive. The ultimate goal would be for students to have all nine options at once and not be overwhelmed.

Special Notes on the Use of These Menus

- These menus give students the opportunity to create commercials and news reports ● ■. Although students enjoy producing their own videos, there often are difficulties obtaining the equipment and scheduling the use of a video recorder. This activity can be modified by allowing students to act out the product (like a play) or, if students have the technology, allowing them to produce a webcam version of their presentation.
- The triangle menu ▲ asks students to use recycled materials to create their diorama. This does not mean only plastic and paper; instead, students should focus on using materials in new ways. It works well if a box is started for "recycled" contributions at the beginning of the school year. That way, students always have access to these types of materials.
- The square menu ■ allows students to create a bulletin board display. Some classrooms may only have one bulletin board, so the teacher can divide the board into sections, or additional classroom wall or hall space can be sectioned off for the creation of these displays. Students can plan their display based on the amount of space they are assigned.

Time Frame

- 2–3 weeks—Students are given the menu as the unit is started. As the teacher presents lessons throughout the week, he or she should refer back to the menu options associated with that content. The teacher will go over all of the options for that content and have students place check marks in the boxes that represent the activities they are most interested in completing. As students choose activities, they should complete a column or a row. When students complete this pattern, they have completed one activity from each content area, learning style, or level of Bloom's revised taxonomy, depending on the design of the menu.
- 1 week—At the start of the unit, the teacher chooses the three activities he or she feels are most valuable for students. Stations can be set up in the class-

room. These three activities are available for student choice throughout the week as regular instruction takes place.

- 1–2 days—The teacher chooses an activity from the menu to use with the entire class.

Suggested Forms

- All-purpose rubric
- Student presentation rubric
- Free-choice proposal form

A Farewell to Arms

Directions: Choose one activity each for breakfast, lunch, and dinner. Dessert is an activity you can choose to do after you have finished your other meals. All products must be completed by: _____.

Breakfast

❑ Make a set of trading cards for the main characters in the story. Include at least one quote that describes each character.

❑ Select one of the description passages of the war and create a diorama to show what is written.

❑ Use a Venn diagram to compare Lieutenant Henry with Ettore Moretti. Include quotes for each character.

Lunch

❑ Design a timeline that documents the major events that take place between Catherine and Henry.

❑ Complete a story map for *A Farewell to Arms*.

❑ Free choice: Submit a free choice proposal about the events in *A Farewell to Arms* to your teacher for approval.

Dinner

❑ Prepare a speech to convince others that *A Farewell to Arms* is a book about love rather than war.

❑ Select one event that could have changed the story if the characters had access to the medicine we have today. Rewrite the event with the new outcome based on the new medicine.

❑ Using a windowpane, record at least five quotes you read in the story that are meaningful to you. Explain why each is meaningful.

Dessert

❑ Record a commercial that could have been used to convince other Americans to join the Italian army.

❑ Design a crossword puzzle about the events and characters found in *A Farewell to Arms*.

A Farewell to Arms

Directions: Check the boxes you plan to complete. They should form a tic-tac-toe across or down. All products are due by: _____.

☐ **Modern-Day Medicine** Medicine has changed significantly since World War I. Keep a medical diary in which you note any medical idea or procedure mentioned in the story that is now diagnosed and treated differently.	☐ **Love and War** Decide if *A Farewell to Arms* is a story about love or war. Using quotes and facts from the story, prepare a PowerPoint presentation to convince others of your opinion.	☐ **The Quotes** Make a collection of at least 10 quotes from this story that are meaningful to you. Record each quote in a scrapbook, providing a brief explanation about why you selected it.
☐ **The News** Prepare a news report that covers the retreat described in Book Three. Your report should include an interview with a character of your choice.	☐ **Free Choice:** *On the Setting of A Farewell to Arms* (Fill out your proposal form before beginning the free choice!)	☐ **Love and War** Design a timeline that documents how Henry and Catherine's love changes over time. Include one quote for each event on your timeline.
☐ **Love and War** Henry responds to the war and its impact on his life in unique ways. Design a Venn diagram that compares Henry's outlook to others fighting in the war. Include quotes for all areas of your diagram.	☐ **The Characters** Create a large windowpane to record information about each character who interacts with Lieutenant Henry. Include at least one quote for each character that describes him or her.	☐ **We Need You!** Record a commercial that uses the reasons why Henry joined the Italian army to convince other Americans to join foreign armies.

Name: _____

A Farewell to Arms

Directions: Check the boxes you plan to complete. They should form a tic-tac-toe across or down. All products are due by: _____.

☐ **Modern-Day Medicine** Select two of the illnesses discussed in this story and create a brochure for each that shares their prevention, cause, and treatment based on present-day medicine.	☐ **Love and War** Decide if *A Farewell to Arms* is a story about love or war. Using quotes and examples from the story, prepare a persuasive speech to convince others of your opinion.	☐ **The Quotes** Lieutenant Henry uses quotes, written passages, and universal ideas from other great writers. Record each in a scrapbook, documenting its origin and how it applies to the events in *A Farewell to Arms*.
☐ **The News** Prepare a news report that covers the retreat described in Book Three. In addition to the basic description of the retreat, it must also address the emotions it is creating by interviewing a character of your choice.	☐ **Free Choice:** *On the Setting of A Farewell to Arms* (Fill out your proposal form before beginning the free choice!)	☐ **Love and War** Design a three-dimensional timeline that documents how Henry and Catherine's love changes over time. Include at least one quote for each event on your timeline.
☐ **Love and War** Keep a diary for Henry as he progresses through the book. Create an entry for each significant war-related event that takes place. Each entry should begin with a well-chosen quote from Henry.	☐ **The Characters** Design a bulletin board display that shares information about each character. Include at least two quotes for each character, one in which Henry describes the character, and another that shows how the character impacts him.	☐ **We Need You!** Think about why Henry joined the Italian army. Record a commercial that could be used to convince more Americans to join a foreign army.

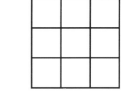

Hamlet

Meal Menu ▲ *and Tic-Tac-Toe Menu* ● ■

Reading Objectives Covered Through These Menus and These Activities

- Students will represent textual evidence and use it to prove conclusions.
- Students will make and explain inferences made from the story.
- Students will analyze the various literary aspects of a story.
- Students will compare different forms of a written work (written versus performed).
- Students will analyze characters, their relationships, and their importance in the story.
- Students will recognize and analyze story plot and problem resolution.

Writing Objectives Covered Through These Menus and These Activities

- Students will write to express their feelings, inform, explain, describe, narrate, entertain, develop, influence, persuade, reflect, or problem solve.
- Students will support their responses with textual evidence.
- Students will exhibit voice in their writing.

Materials Needed by Students for Completion

- *Hamlet* by William Shakespeare
- Poster board or large white paper
- Microsoft PowerPoint or other slideshow software
- Ruler (for comic strips) ▲ ●
- DVD or VHS recorder (for news reports ▲ ■, videos ●)
- Internet access (for WebQuest) ●
- Blank index cards (for trading cards) ■

Special Notes on the Modifications of These Menus

- This topic has two different menu formats: The Meal menu ▲ and Tic-Tac-Toe ● ■ menu. The Meal menu is specifically selected for the triangle ▲ option as it easily allows the menu to be broken into manageable bits; the different meals separate the page, making it less daunting for special needs students. The space between the meals makes it easy for the teacher to cut the menu as needed based on the comfort level of the students. If it is the first time choice is being introduced, then the children may receive only the strip of the top breakfast options. Then, when they have finished one of those options, they can receive a strip of lunches and finally, the enrichment-level dinner and dessert activities. After students have grown more accustomed to making choices, the menu might be cut just once after the lunch options, so students can select a breakfast and a lunch and submit them to the teacher. Then, they can choose from the dinner strip they receive. The ultimate goal would be for students to have all nine options at once and not be overwhelmed.

Special Notes on the Use of These Menus

- These menus give students the opportunity to create a news report ▲ ■ or video ●. Although students enjoy producing their own videos, there often are difficulties obtaining the equipment and scheduling the use of a video recorder. This activity can be modified by allowing students to act out the product (like a play) or, if students have the technology, allowing them to produce a webcam version of their presentation.
- The circle menu ● allows students to create a WebQuest. There are multiple versions and templates for WebQuests available on the Internet. Teachers should decide whether to specify a certain format or allow students to create one of their own choosing.

Time Frame

- 2–3 weeks—Students are given the menu as the unit is started. As the teacher presents lessons throughout the week, he or she should refer back to the menu options associated with that content. The teacher will go over all of the options for that content and have students place check marks in the boxes that represent the activities they are most interested in completing. As students choose activities, they should complete a column or a row. When students complete this pattern, they have completed one activity from each content area, learning style, or level of Bloom's revised taxonomy, depending on the design of the menu.
- 1 week—At the start of the unit, the teacher chooses the three activities he or she feels are most valuable for students. Stations can be set up in the classroom. These three activities are available for student choice throughout the week as regular instruction takes place.
- 1–2 days—The teacher chooses an activity from the menu to use with the entire class.

Suggested Forms

- All-purpose rubric
- Student presentation rubric
- Free-choice proposal form

Hamlet

Directions: Choose one activity each for breakfast, lunch, and dinner. Dessert is an activity you can choose to do after you have finished your other meals. All products must be completed by: _____.

Breakfast

☐ Create a social media page for Hamlet. His page needs to have at least five posts and check-ins that relate to the play.

☐ Design a windowpane with a drawing of each character in *Hamlet*.

☐ Create a comic strip that features all of the characters in *Hamlet*.

Lunch

☐ Act out *Hamlet* using a new ending.

☐ Reenact the famous skull scene using modern-day language.

☐ Perform a news report that shares the important events that take place at the end of *Hamlet*.

Dinner

☐ Select one of the important scenes from *Hamlet* and rewrite the dialogue using modern terms and language. This "translation" should be your own and not taken from another source.

☐ Prepare a poster that shares at least three examples of modern movies that are similar to *Hamlet*.

☐ Free choice: Submit a free choice proposal about a modern-day interpretation of Hamlet to your teacher for approval.

Dessert

☐ Watch a movie version of *Hamlet*. Use a Venn diagram to compare and contrast the movie and the written play.

☐ Consider possible explanations for Hamlet and Ophelia's mental health problems. Create a PowerPoint presentation that shares your findings.

Name: _____

Hamlet

Directions: Check the boxes you plan to complete. They should form a tic-tac-toe across or down. All products are due by: _____.

☐ Modern-Day *Hamlet*	☐ The Plot Thickens	☐ The Characters
Prepare a PowerPoint presentation that shares at least three examples of modern movies that are similar to *Hamlet*. Your presentation should focus on the themes and contain quotes to support your selection.	Select an important event that impacts the end of this play and change the event. Make a video in which you share how the play progresses from that point forward.	Create a social media page for Ophelia. Her page needs to have at least seven posts and check-ins that follow the events in *Hamlet*.
☐ The Characters	☐ **Free Choice:** *On Modern-Day* **Hamlet** (Fill out your proposal form before beginning the free choice!)	☐ The Plot Thickens
Watch a movie version of *Hamlet*. Write a newspaper article that discusses the actors who were selected to play each character. Include whether you believe each part was well cast.		Create a WebQuest that has questors visiting sites to learn more about the Prince of Denmark and the history behind the events that were taking place during this play.
☐ The Plot Thickens	☐ The Characters	☐ Modern-Day *Hamlet*
Create a comic strip that summarizes and depicts the important events in each act of *Hamlet*.	Design a windowpane with a drawing of each character in *Hamlet*. Include one quote from the play to support your drawing.	Reenact the famous skull scene for your classmates using modern-day language and references.

Name: _____ ■

Hamlet

Directions: Check the boxes you plan to complete. They should form a tic-tac-toe across or down. All products are due by: _____.

☐ **Modern-Day *Hamlet*** Select one of the important scenes from *Hamlet* and rewrite the dialogue using modern terms and language. This "translation" should be your own and not taken from another source.	☐ **The Plot Thickens** Select an important event that impacts the end of this play. Reenact the play from that point forward sharing your new ending.	☐ **The Characters** Create a social media page for one of the characters in the play. Your page needs to have at least 10 posts or check-ins that follow the events in *Hamlet*. Your posts should also include comments from other characters.
☐ **The Characters** Consider possible explanations for Hamlet and Ophelia's mental health problems. After determining possible causes, create a PowerPoint presentation that could used to educate them on possible treatments.	☐ **Free Choice:** *On Modern-Day* Hamlet (Fill out your proposal form before beginning the free choice!)	☐ **The Plot Thickens** Pretend that *Hamlet* is being turned into a musical. Select at least four modern-day songs that could be used in the new production. Present your creation to the class.
☐ **The Plot Thickens** Record a news report that shares the important events that take place at the end of *Hamlet*.	☐ **The Characters** Make a set of trading cards for the different characters in *Hamlet*. Include information about each based on descriptions provided in the play.	☐ **Modern-Day *Hamlet*** Reenact the famous skull scene for your classmates using modern-day language and references.

A Raisin in the Sun

20-50-80 Menu

Reading Objectives Covered Through These Menus and These Activities

- Students will represent textual evidence and use it to prove conclusions.
- Students will make and explain inferences made from the story.
- Students will analyze the various literary aspects of a story.
- Students will represent textual evidence by using story maps.
- Students will analyze characters, their relationships, and their importance in the story.
- Students will recognize and analyze story plot and problem resolution.

Writing Objectives Covered Through These Menus and These Activities

- Students will write to express their feelings, inform, explain, describe, narrate, entertain, persuade, reflect, or problem solve.
- Students will support their responses with textual evidence.

Materials Needed by Students for Completion

- *A Raisin in the Sun* by Lorraine Hansberry
- Poster board or large white paper
- Recycled materials (for dioramas) ▲ ●
- Microsoft PowerPoint or other slideshow software ■
- Magazines (for collages) ▲ ●
- DVD or VHS recorder (for videos) ● ■

Special Notes on the Modifications of These Menus

- If needed, further modifications can be made to a 20-50-80 menu based on the needs of your students. The easiest modification is altering the point goal from 100; lowering or raising the goal on a menu by 10 (or 20) points is appropriate if additional modification up or down is needed.

Special Notes on the Use of These Menus

- The circle ● and square ■ menus give students the opportunity to create a video. Although students enjoy producing their own videos, there often are difficulties obtaining the equipment and scheduling the use of a video recorder. This activity can be modified by allowing students to act out the product (like a play) or, if students have the technology, allowing them to produce a webcam version of their presentation.

- The triangle ▲ and circle ● menus ask students to use recycled materials to create their dioramas. This does not mean only plastic and paper; instead, students should focus on using materials in new ways. It works well if a box is started for "recycled" contributions at the beginning of the school year. That way, students always have access to these types of materials.

Time Frame

- 1–2 weeks—Students are given a menu as the unit is started, and the teacher discusses all of the product options on the menu. As the different options are discussed, students will choose the activities they are most interested in completing so they meet their goal of 100 points. As the lessons progress through the week(s), the teacher and students refer back to the menu options associated with the content being taught.
- 1–2 days—The teacher chooses an activity or product from the menu to use with the entire class.

Suggested Forms

- All-purpose rubric
- Student presentation rubric
- Proposal form for point-based projects

A Raisin in the Sun

Directions: Choose at least two activities from the options below. The activities must total 100 points. Place a checkmark next to each box to show which activities you will complete. All activities must be completed by: _____.

20 points

❑ Create an acrostic for the word *dreams*. Write one of your dreams for each letter.

❑ Make a poster that shows why this play is called *A Raisin in the Sun*.

50 points

❑ Design a diorama for the set of *A Raisin in the Sun*.

❑ Make a mind map that shares what each family member believes should be done with the check, as well as why he or she believes that use would be the best.

❑ Create a collage of quotes from the play that tells about each character. Label each quote with the character it describes.

❑ Free choice: Submit a proposal form for a product of your choice.

80 points

❑ When the play finishes, there are still a few questions in the audiences' minds. Write another act for the play in which Beneatha chooses to go to Africa with Joseph or stays at home with Mama.

❑ After reading *A Raisin in the Sun*, watch a movie presentation of the play. Perform a speech in which you compare the two works.

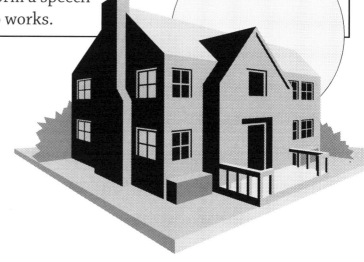

A Raisin in the Sun

Directions: Choose at least two activities from the options below. The activities must total 100 points. Place a checkmark next to each box to show which activities you will complete. All activities must be completed by: _____.

20 points

❐ Create an acrostic for the word *dreams*. Write one of your dreams for each letter.

❐ Design a diorama of the set of *A Raisin in the Sun*.

50 points

❐ Make a mind map that shares what each family member believes should be done with the check, as well as why he or she believes that use would be the best.

❐ Create a collage of quotes from the play that shows the importance of money. Include an explanation for each quote.

❐ After reading *A Raisin in the Sun*, watch a movie presentation of the play. Write an essay to compare the two works.

❐ Free choice: Submit a proposal form for a product of your choice.

80 points

❐ When the play finishes, there are still a few questions in the audiences' minds. Write another act for the play that follows Beneatha and the outcome from the important choice she has to make.

❐ Mama's plant is considered one of the most important symbols in this play. Record a video in which you agree or disagree with this idea. Support your opinion with quotes from the play.

A Raisin in the Sun

Directions: Choose at least two activities from the options below. The activities must total 100 points. Place a checkmark next to each box to show which activities you will complete. All activities must be completed by: _____.

20 points

☐ Create a picture dictionary for words that are unique to stage directions. Include examples from *A Raisin in the Sun*.

☐ Make a mind map that shares what each family member believes should be done with the check, as well as why he or she believes that use would be the best.

50 points

☐ After reading *A Raisin in the Sun*, watch a movie presentation of the play. Use a Venn diagram to compare the two works and then create an advertisement for the original work.

☐ Consider which character changes the most as the play progresses. Develop a PowerPoint presentation that shares how he or she changes. Prove your findings using quotes from the play.

☐ Mama's plant is considered one of the most important symbols in this play. Record a video in which you agree or disagree with this idea. Support your opinion with quotes from the play.

☐ Free choice: Submit a proposal form for a product of your choice.

80 points

☐ When the play finishes, there are still a few questions in the audiences' minds. Write another act for the play that follows Beneatha and the outcome from the important choice she has to make.

☐ Mr. Lindner and the Clybourne Park Improvement Association have certain beliefs about the Youngers moving into Clybourne. Write a research paper about the time period of this play and thoughts surrounding their beliefs.

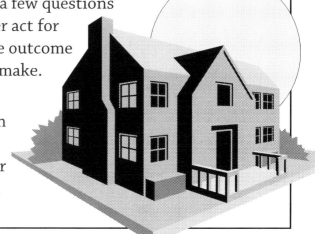

CHAPTER 6

Poetry

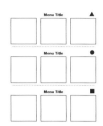

"Sonnet 73"

Poetry Shape Menu

Reading Objectives Covered Through These Menus and These Activities

- Students will compare one literary work with another.
- Students will interpret figurative language and multiple meaning words.
- Students will make predictions based on what is read.
- Students will use resources and references to build meaning.

Writing Objectives Covered Through These Menus and These Activities

- Students will write to express their feelings, reflect, inform, explain, describe, or narrate.
- Students will use vivid language.
- Students will exhibit voice in their writing.

Materials Needed by Students for Completion

- "Sonnet 73" by William Shakespeare (see p. 154)
- Poster board or large white paper
- Blank index cards (for concentration cards) ▲
- Ruler (for comic strips) ●
- DVD or VHS recorder (for videos) ▲
- Microsoft PowerPoint or other slideshow software ■

Special Notes on the Modifications of These Menus

- This menu is unique from the others as teachers can select the number of choices based on the amount of time they plan to spend processing a particular poem. This menu is divided into three sections: The top or triangle section ▲ has activities with the most modifications, the middle or circle section ● has activities with minor modifications, and the lower or square section ■ has activities that offer the most extension. If the goal is to have students create one product for the poem, then the teacher can provide each student with a strip of an appropriate level of options. For a more in-depth study, the teacher can provide the entire menu and students select one option from each section of the menu.

Special Notes on the Use of These Menus

- The triangle strip ▲ of this menu gives students the opportunity to create a video. Although students enjoy producing their own videos, there often are difficulties obtaining the equipment and scheduling the use of a video recorder. This activity can be modified by allowing students to act out the product (like a play) or, if students have the technology, allowing them to produce a webcam version of their product.
- The square strip ■ of this menu allows students to create a bulletin board display. Some classrooms may only have one bulletin board, so the teacher can divide the board into sections, or additional classroom wall or hall space can be sectioned off for the creation of these displays. Students can plan their display based on the amount of space they are assigned.

Time Frame

- 1 week—Students are given the menu before the poem is read. The teacher will go over all of the options for the menu and have students indicate each option that represents the activity they are most interested in completing. The teacher may assign the menu as independent work or choose to allow students time to work after other work is finished.
- 1–2 days—The teacher chooses a strip for each student to complete based on his or her specific needs. The student selects one of the activities on the strip and works on it for independent practice.

Suggested Forms

- All-purpose rubric
- Student presentation rubric
- Free-choice proposal form

Sonnet 73

by William Shakespeare

That time of year thou mayst in me behold
When yellow leaves, or none, or few, do hang
Upon those boughs which shake against the cold,
Bare ruin'd choirs, where late the sweet birds sang.
In me thou seest the twilight of such day
As after sunset fadeth in the west,
Which by and by black night doth take away,
Death's second self, that seals up all in rest.
In me thou see'st the glowing of such fire
That on the ashes of his youth doth lie,
As the death-bed whereon it must expire
Consumed with that which it was nourish'd by.
   This thou perceivest, which makes thy love more strong,
   To love that well which thou must leave ere long.

"Sonnet 73"

Directions: Select one of the following options.   ▲

Make a set
of metaphor
concentration cards
to match words in
the poem with their
real meaning.

Using a poster format,
draw a picture that
represents the tone
of this sonnet.

Record a video of
yourself doing a
dramatic reading
of "Sonnet 73."

- -

"Sonnet 73"

Directions: Select one of the following options.   ●

Create a comic
strip that shows
the four events the
speaker describes
in each quatrain
of this sonnet.

Read another one
of Shakespeare's
sonnets that has a
different tone. Use
a Venn diagram
to compare the
two poems.

Free choice:
Submit a free choice
proposal about
"Sonnet 73" to your
teacher for approval.

- -

"Sonnet 73"

Directions: Select one of the following options.   ■

Write your own
sonnet that uses
metaphors in the
style of Shakespeare.

Prepare a PowerPoint
presentation that
analyzes a modern-day
sonnet of your choice.

Design a bulletin
board display that
analyzes the rhyme
scheme, rhythm, and
use of metaphors
in "Sonnet 73."

"The Raven"

Poetry Shape Menu

Reading Objectives Covered Through These Menus and These Activities

- Students will compare one literary work with another.
- Students will interpret figurative language and multiple meaning words.
- Students will make predictions based on what is read.
- Students will use resources and references to build meaning.

Writing Objectives Covered Through These Menus and These Activities

- Students will write to express their feelings, reflect, inform, explain, describe, or narrate.
- Students will use vivid language.
- Students will exhibit voice in their writing.

Materials Needed by Students for Completion

- "The Raven" by Edgar Allan Poe (see p. 158)
- Poster board or large white paper
- Magazines (for collages) ▲
- Microsoft PowerPoint or other slideshow software ■
- Internet access (for YouTube) ■
- DVD or VHS recorder (for commercials) ■

Special Notes on the Modifications of These Menus

- This menu is unique from the others as teachers can select the number of choices based on the amount of time they plan to spend processing a particular poem. This menu is divided into three sections: The top or triangle section ▲ has activities with the most modifications, the middle or circle section ● has activities with minor modifications, and the lower or square section ■ has activities that offer the most extension. If the goal is to have students create one product for the poem, then the teacher can provide each student with a strip of an appropriate level of options. For a more in-depth study, the teacher can provide the entire menu and students select one option from each section of the menu.

Special Notes on the Use of This Menu

- None

Time Frame

- 1 week—Students are given the menu before the poem is read. The teacher will go over all of the options for the menu and have students indicate each option that represents the activity they are most interested in completing. The teacher may assign the menu as independent work or choose to allow students time to work after other work is finished.
- 1–2 days—The teacher chooses a strip for each student to complete based on his or her specific needs. The student selects one of the activities on the strip and works on it for independent practice.

Suggested Forms

- All-purpose rubric
- Student presentation rubric
- Free-choice proposal form

The Raven

by Edgar Allan Poe

Once upon a midnight dreary, while I pondered weak and weary,
Over many a quaint and curious volume of forgotten lore,
While I nodded, nearly napping, suddenly there came a tapping,
As of some one gently rapping, rapping at my chamber door.
'Tis some visitor,' I muttered, 'tapping at my chamber door—
Only this, and nothing more.'

Ah, distinctly I remember it was in the bleak December,
And each separate dying ember wrought its ghost upon the floor.
Eagerly I wished the morrow;—vainly I had sought to borrow
From my books surcease of sorrow—sorrow for the lost Lenore—
For the rare and radiant maiden whom the angels name Lenore—
Nameless here for evermore.

And the silken sad uncertain rustling of each purple curtain
Thrilled me—filled me with fantastic terrors never felt before;
So that now, to still the beating of my heart, I stood repeating
'Tis some visitor entreating entrance at my chamber door—
Some late visitor entreating entrance at my chamber door;—
This it is, and nothing more,'

Presently my soul grew stronger; hesitating then no longer,
'Sir,' said I, 'or Madam, truly your forgiveness I implore;
But the fact is I was napping, and so gently you came rapping,
And so faintly you came tapping, tapping at my chamber door,
That I scarce was sure I heard you'—here I opened wide the door;—
Darkness there, and nothing more.

Deep into that darkness peering, long I stood there wondering, fearing,
Doubting, dreaming dreams no mortal ever dared to dream before;
But the silence was unbroken, and the darkness gave no token,
And the only word there spoken was the whispered word, 'Lenore!'
This I whispered, and an echo murmured back the word, 'Lenore!'
Merely this and nothing more.

Back into the chamber turning, all my soul within me burning,
Soon again I heard a tapping somewhat louder than before.

'Surely,' said I, 'surely that is something at my window lattice;
Let me see then, what threat is, and this mystery explore—
Let my heart be still a moment and this mystery explore;—
'Tis the wind and nothing more!'

Open here I flung the shutter, when, with many a flirt and flutter,
In there stepped a stately raven of the saintly days of yore.
Not the least obeisance made he; not a minute stopped or stayed he;
But, with mien of lord or lady, perched above my chamber door—
Perched upon a bust of Pallas just above my chamber door—
Perched, and sat, and nothing more.

Then this ebony bird beguiling my sad fancy into smiling,
By the grave and stern decorum of the countenance it wore,
'Though thy crest be shorn and shaven, thou,' I said, 'art sure no craven.
Ghastly grim and ancient raven wandering from the nightly shore—
Tell me what thy lordly name is on the Night's Plutonian shore!'
Quoth the raven, 'Nevermore.'

Much I marvelled this ungainly fowl to hear discourse so plainly,
Though its answer little meaning—little relevancy bore;
For we cannot help agreeing that no living human being
Ever yet was blessed with seeing bird above his chamber door—
Bird or beast above the sculptured bust above his chamber door,
With such name as 'Nevermore.'

But the raven, sitting lonely on the placid bust, spoke only,
That one word, as if his soul in that one word he did outpour.
Nothing further then he uttered—not a feather then he fluttered—
Till I scarcely more than muttered 'Other friends have flown before—
On the morrow he will leave me, as my hopes have flown before.'
Then the bird said, 'Nevermore.'

Startled at the stillness broken by reply so aptly spoken,
'Doubtless,' said I, 'what it utters is its only stock and store,
Caught from some unhappy master whom unmerciful disaster
Followed fast and followed faster till his songs one burden bore—
Till the dirges of his hope that melancholy burden bore
Of "Never-nevermore."

But the raven still beguiling all my sad soul into smiling,
Straight I wheeled a cushioned seat in front of bird and bust and door;
Then, upon the velvet sinking, I betook myself to linking
Fancy unto fancy, thinking what this ominous bird of yore—
What this grim, ungainly, ghastly, gaunt, and ominous bird of yore
Meant in croaking 'Nevermore.'

This I sat engaged in guessing, but no syllable expressing
To the fowl whose fiery eyes now burned into my bosom's core;
This and more I sat divining, with my head at ease reclining
On the cushion's velvet lining that the lamp-light gloated o'er,
But whose velvet violet lining with the lamp-light gloating o'er,
She shall press, ah, nevermore!

Then, methought, the air grew denser, perfumed from an unseen censer
Swung by Seraphim whose foot-falls tinkled on the tufted floor.
'Wretch,' I cried, 'thy God hath lent thee—by these angels he has sent thee
Respite—respite and nepenthe from thy memories of Lenore!
Quaff, oh quaff this kind nepenthe, and forget this lost Lenore!'
Quoth the raven, 'Nevermore.'

'Prophet!' said I, 'thing of evil!—prophet still, if bird or devil!—
Whether tempter sent, or whether tempest tossed thee here ashore,
Desolate yet all undaunted, on this desert land enchanted—
On this home by horror haunted—tell me truly, I implore—
Is there—*is* there balm in Gilead?— tell me—tell me, I implore!'
Quoth the raven, 'Nevermore.'

'Prophet!' said I, 'thing of evil!—prophet still, if bird or devil!
By that Heaven that bends above us—by that God we both adore—
Tell this soul with sorrow laden if, within the distant Aidenn,
It shall clasp a sainted maiden whom the angels name Lenore—
Clasp a rare and radiant maiden, whom the angels name Lenore?'
Quoth the raven, 'Nevermore.'

'Be that word our sign of parting, bird or fiend!' I shrieked upstarting—
'Get thee back into the tempest and the Night's Plutonian shore!
Leave no black plume as a token of that lie thy soul hath spoken!
Leave my loneliness unbroken!—quit the bust above my door!
Take thy beak from out my heart, and take thy form from off my door!'
Quoth the raven, 'Nevermore.'

And the raven, never flitting, still is sitting, still is sitting
On the pallid bust of Pallas just above my chamber door;
And his eyes have all the seeming of a demon's that is dreaming,
And the lamp-light o'er him streaming throws his shadow on the floor;
And my soul from out that shadow that lies floating on the floor
Shall be lifted—nevermore!

"The Raven"

Directions: Select one of the following options. ▲

Make a picture dictionary for 15 "new to you" vocabulary words found in "The Raven."

Draw a picture of what you think Lenore may have looked like based on Poe's description.

Create a collage of words from the poem that contribute to the tone of the work.

"The Raven"

Directions: Select one of the following options. ●

Make a windowpane of examples of alliteration, assonance, onomatopoeia, personification, and repetition from "The Raven."

Using a copy of "The Raven" and a key you develop, mark the literary devices found in each line.

Free choice: Submit a free choice proposal about the literary devices that are found in "The Raven" to your teacher for approval.

"The Raven"

Directions: Select one of the following options. ■

Rewrite this poem as a short story that begins when the narrator meets Lenore.

Select another poem written by Edgar Allan Poe. Design a PowerPoint presentation that uses both poems to draw conclusions about his poetic style.

Rap and song versions of this poem can be found on YouTube. After listening to at least three different versions, create a commercial for the version you feel best represents the poem.

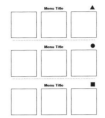

"We Grow Accustomed to the Dark"

Poetry Shape Menu

Reading Objectives Covered Through These Menus and These Activities

- Students will compare one literary work with another.
- Students will interpret figurative language and multiple meaning words.
- Students will make predictions based on what is read.
- Students will use resources and references to build meaning.

Writing Objectives Covered Through These Menus and These Activities

- Students will write to express their feelings, reflect, inform, explain, describe, or narrate.
- Students will use vivid language.
- Students will exhibit voice in their writing.

Materials Needed by Students for Completion

- "We Grow Accustomed to the Dark" by Emily Dickinson (see p. 165)
- Poster board or large white paper
- DVD or VHS recorder (for video) ●
- Recycled materials (for dioramas) ▲
- Scrapbooking materials ■

Special Notes on the Modifications of These Menus

- This menu is unique from the others as teachers can select the number of choices based on the amount of time they plan to spend processing a particular poem. This menu is divided into three sections: The top or triangle section ▲ has activities with the most modifications, the middle or circle section ● has activities with minor modifications, and the lower or square section ■ has activities that offer the most extension. If the goal is to have students create one product for the poem, then the teacher can provide each student with a strip of an appropriate level of options. For a more in-depth study, the teacher can provide the entire menu and students select one option from each section of the menu.

Special Notes on the Use of These Menus

- This menu gives students the opportunity to create a video. Although students enjoy producing their own videos, there often are difficulties obtaining the equipment and scheduling the use of a video recorder. This activity can be modified by allowing students to act out the product (like a play) or, if students have the technology, allowing them to produce a webcam version of their product.
- This menu asks students to use recycled materials to create their diorama. This does not mean only plastic and paper; instead, students should focus on using materials in new ways. It works well if a box is started for "recycled" contributions at the beginning of the school year. That way, students always have access to these types of materials.

Time Frame

- 1 week—Students are given the menu before the poem is read. The teacher will go over all of the options for the menu and have students indicate each option that represents the activity they are most interested in completing. The teacher may assign the menu as independent work or choose to allow students time to work after other work is finished.
- 1–2 days—The teacher chooses a strip for each student to complete based on his or her specific needs. The student selects one of the activities on the strip and works on it for independent practice.

Suggested Forms

- All-purpose rubric
- Student presentation rubric
- Free-choice proposal form

We Grow Accustomed to the Dark
by Emily Dickinson

We grow accustomed to the Dark—
When light is put away—
As when the Neighbor holds the Lamp
To witness her Goodbye—

A Moment—We uncertain step
For newness of the night—
Then—fit our Vision to the Dark—
And meet the Road—erect—

And so of larger—Darkness—
Those Evenings of the Brain—
When not a Moon disclose a sign—
Or Star—come out—within—

The Bravest—grope a little—
And sometimes hit a Tree
Directly in the Forehead—
But as they learn to see—

Either the Darkness alters—
Or something in the sight
Adjusts itself to Midnight—
And Life steps almost straight.

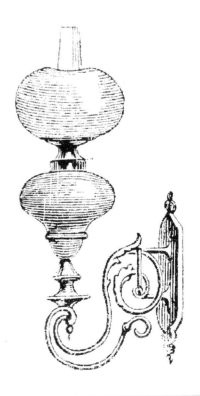

"We Grow Accustomed to the Dark"

Directions: Select one of the following options. ▲

Create
a poster
that shows
possible meanings
for the Dark.

Design
a diorama
to represent
the experience of
"the Bravest."

Make
a
drawing that
illustrates the
meaning of the
poem.

- -

"We Grow Accustomed to the Dark"

Directions: Select one of the following options. ●

Design
a written
class lesson
that analyzes
this poem for its
different
literary
devices.

Record
a video
in which you
use lines from this
poem to prove
if the Dark is
good or
evil.

Free
choice:
Submit
a free choice
proposal for "We
Grow Accustomed
to the Dark."

- -

"We Grow Accustomed to the Dark"

Directions: Select one of the following options. ■

The
message
in this
poem is very
appropriate for
people your age.
Write a letter to Emily
Dickinson explaining
how this poem
"speaks to
you."

Create a
scrapbook of
your personal
experiences with
the Dark.

Select
another
poem with
the same theme as
this one. Write a short
essay that compares
and contrasts the
two poems.

"Ode on a Grecian Urn"

Poetry Shape Menu

Reading Objectives Covered Through These Menus and These Activities

- Students will compare one literary work with another.
- Students will interpret figurative language and multiple meaning words.
- Students will make predictions based on what is read.
- Students will use resources and references to build meaning.

Writing Objectives Covered Through These Menus and These Activities

- Students will write to express their feelings, reflect, inform, explain, describe, or narrate.
- Students will use vivid language.
- Students will exhibit voice in their writing.

Materials Needed by Students for Completion

- "Ode on a Grecian Urn" by John Keats (see p. 169)
- Poster board or large white paper
- Blank index cards (for concentration cards) ▲
- Graph paper or Internet access (for crossword puzzles) ▲

Special Notes on the Modifications of These Menus

- This menu is unique from the others as teachers can select the number of choices based on the amount of time they plan to spend processing a particular poem. This menu is divided into three sections: The top or triangle section ▲ has activities with the most modifications, the middle or circle section ● has activities with minor modifications, and the lower or square section ■ has activities that offer the most extension. If the goal is to have students create one product for the poem, then the teacher can provide each student with a strip of an appropriate level of options. For a more in-depth study, the teacher can provide the entire menu and students select one option from each section of the menu.

Time Frame

- 1 week—Students are given the menu before the poem is read. The teacher will go over all of the options for the menu and have students indicate each option that represents the activity they are most interested in completing. The teacher may assign the menu as independent work or choose to allow students time to work after other work is finished.

- 1–2 days—The teacher chooses a strip for each student to complete based on his or her specific needs. The student selects one of the activities on the strip and works on it for independent practice.

Suggested Forms

- All-purpose rubric
- Student presentation rubric
- Free-choice proposal form

Ode on a Grecian Urn

by John Keats

Thou still unravish'd bride of quietness,
    Thou foster-child of silence and slow time,
Sylvan historian, who canst thus express
    A flowery tale more sweetly than our rhyme:
What leaf-fring'd legend haunts about thy shape
    Of deities or mortals, or of both,
        In Tempe or the dales of Arcady?
    What men or gods are these? What maidens loth?
What mad pursuit? What struggle to escape?
    What pipes and timbrels? What wild ecstasy?

Heard melodies are sweet, but those unheard
    Are sweeter; therefore, ye soft pipes, play on;
Not to the sensual ear, but, more endear'd,
    Pipe to the spirit ditties of no tone:
Fair youth, beneath the trees, thou canst not leave
    Thy song, nor ever can those trees be bare;
        Bold Lover, never, never canst thou kiss,
Though winning near the goal yet, do not grieve;
    She cannot fade, though thou hast not thy bliss,
        For ever wilt thou love, and she be fair!

Ah, happy, happy boughs! that cannot shed
    Your leaves, nor ever bid the Spring adieu;
And, happy melodist, unwearied,
    For ever piping songs for ever new;
More happy love! more happy, happy love!
    For ever warm and still to be enjoy'd,
        For ever panting, and for ever young;
All breathing human passion far above,
    That leaves a heart high-sorrowful and cloy'd,
        A burning forehead, and a parching tongue.

Who are these coming to the sacrifice?
　　To what green altar, O mysterious priest,
Lead'st thou that heifer lowing at the skies,
　　And all her silken flanks with garlands drest?
What little town by river or sea shore,
　　Or mountain-built with peaceful citadel,
　　　　Is emptied of this folk, this pious morn?
And, little town, thy streets for evermore
　　Will silent be; and not a soul to tell
　　　　Why thou art desolate, can e'er return.

O Attic shape! Fair attitude! with brede
　　Of marble men and maidens overwrought,
With forest branches and the trodden weed;
　　Thou, silent form, dost tease us out of thought
As doth eternity: Cold Pastoral!
　　When old age shall this generation waste,
　　　　Thou shalt remain, in midst of other woe
Than ours, a friend to man, to whom thou say'st,
　　"Beauty is truth, truth beauty,—that is all
　　　　Ye know on earth, and all ye need to know."

Name: _____

"Ode on a Grecian Urn"

Directions: Select one of the following options. ▲

Draw a representation of the urn including its shape and the different pictures impressed on it.

Create a set of concentration cards to match each of the writer's contractions with the word(s) it represents.

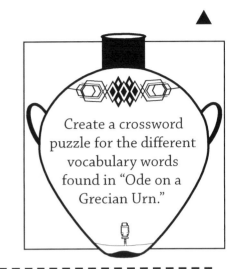
Create a crossword puzzle for the different vocabulary words found in "Ode on a Grecian Urn."

"Ode on a Grecian Urn"

Directions: Select one of the following options. ●

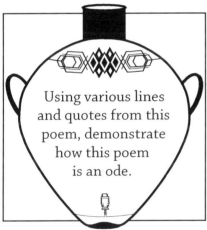
Using various lines and quotes from this poem, demonstrate how this poem is an ode.

Create a poster that shows the different literary devices found in this poem.

Free choice: Submit a free choice proposal about the literary structures and technical devices found in "Ode on a Grecian Urn."

"Ode on a Grecian Urn"

Directions: Select one of the following options. ■

Select one of the pictures that Keats describes. Write the story behind what is happening in the picture.

Choose another piece of literature in which someone speaks to an inanimate object. Write an essay to discuss the benefits shown in both works.

Research a museum artifact that has survived many generations and write an ode about what the object tells us.

"Song of Myself"

Poetry Shape Menu

Reading Objectives Covered Through These Menus and These Activities

- Students will compare one literary work with another.
- Students will interpret figurative language.
- Students will make predictions based on what is read.
- Students will use resources and references to build meaning.

Writing Objectives Covered Through These Menus and These Activities

- Students will write to express their feelings, reflect, inform, explain, describe, or narrate.
- Students will use vivid language.
- Students will exhibit voice in their writing.

Materials Needed by Students for Completion

- "Song of Myself" by Walt Whitman (see http://www.poetryfoundation.org/poem/174745)
- Poster board or large white paper
- Ruler (for comic strips) ▲
- Internet access (for WebQuest) ●
- Blank index cards (for concentration cards) ●
- DVD or VHS recorder (for videos) ■

Special Notes on the Modifications of These Menus

- This menu is unique from the others as teachers can select the number of choices based on the amount of time they plan to spend processing a particular poem. This menu is divided into three sections: The top or triangle section ▲ has activities with the most modifications, the middle or circle section ● has activities with minor modifications, and the lower or square section ■ has activities that offer the most extension. If the goal is to have students create one product for the poem, then the teacher can provide each student with a strip of an appropriate level of options. For a more in-depth study, the teacher can provide the entire menu and students select one option from each section of the menu.

Special Notes on the Use of These Menus

- The square strip ■ of this menu gives students the opportunity to create a video. Although students enjoy producing their own videos, there often are difficulties obtaining the equipment and scheduling the use of a video recorder. This activity can be modified by allowing students to act out the product (like a play) or, if students have the technology, allowing them to produce a webcam version of their product.
- The circle strip ● of this menu allows students to create a WebQuest. There are multiple versions and templates for WebQuests available on the Internet. Teachers should decide whether to specify a certain format or allow students to create one of their own choosing.

Time Frame

- 1 week—Students are given the menu before the poem is read. The teacher will go over all of the options for the menu and have students indicate each option that represents the activity they are most interested in completing. The teacher may assign the menu as independent work or choose to allow students time to work after other work is finished.
- 1–2 days—The teacher chooses a strip for each student to complete based on his or her specific needs. The student selects one of the activities on the strip and works on it for independent practice.

Suggested Forms

- All-purpose rubric
- Student presentation rubric
- Free-choice proposal form

"Song of Myself"

Directions: Select one of the following options.   ▲

Draw a comic strip that illustrates a story contained within "Song of Myself."

Design an acrostic for the word *myself* using quotes from the poem.

Create a book cover for the book that contains "Song of Myself."

"Song of Myself"

Directions: Select one of the following options.   ●

Create a WebQuest that could be used to teach others about Walt Whitman and his other works.

Read two additional poems by Walt Whitman. Use these three poems to create a bulletin board display about his style and use of literary devices.

Create a set of concentration cards to match objects in the poem with their deeper (and often historic) meanings.

"Song of Myself"

Directions: Select one of the following options.   ■

Come to school as Walt Whitman and discuss your reasons for writing this epic poem.

Make a video for one of the sections of "Song of Myself" that shares its modern-day applications.

Free choice: Submit a free choice proposal about how "Song of Myself" applies to your daily life.

"Mending Wall"

Poetry Shape Menu

Reading Objectives Covered Through These Menus and These Activities

- Students will compare one literary work with another.
- Students will interpret figurative language and multiple meaning words.
- Students will make predictions based on what is read.
- Students will use resources and references to build meaning.

Writing Objectives Covered Through These Menus and These Activities

- Students will write to express their feelings, reflect, inform, explain, describe, or narrate.
- Students will use vivid language.
- Students will exhibit voice in their writing.

Materials Needed by Students for Completion

- "Mending Wall" by Robert Frost (see p. 177)
- Poster board or large white paper
- Magazines (for collages) ●
- DVD or VHS recorder (for documentary) ■
- Scrapbooking materials ■

Special Notes on the Modifications of These Menus

- This menu is unique from the others as teachers can select the number of choices based on the amount of time they plan to spend processing a particular poem. This menu is divided into three sections: The top or triangle section ▲ has activities with the most modifications, the middle or circle section ● has activities with minor modifications, and the lower or square section ■ has activities that offer the most extension. If the goal is to have students create one product for the poem, then the teacher can provide each student with a strip of an appropriate level of options. For a more in-depth study, the teacher can provide the entire menu and students select one option from each section of the menu.

Special Notes on the Use of These Menus

- This menu gives students the opportunity to create a documentary. Although students enjoy producing their own videos, there often are difficulties obtaining the equipment and scheduling the use of a video recorder. This activity can be modified by allowing students to act out the product (like a play) or, if students have the technology, allowing them to produce a webcam version of their product.

Time Frame

- 1 week—Students are given the menu before the poem is read. The teacher will go over all of the options for the menu and have students indicate each option that represents the activity they are most interested in completing. The teacher may assign the menu as independent work or choose to allow students time to work after other work is finished.
- 1–2 days—The teacher chooses a strip for each student to complete based on his or her specific needs. The student selects one of the activities on the strip and works on it for independent practice.

Suggested Forms

- All-purpose rubric
- Student presentation rubric
- Free-choice proposal form

Mending Wall

by Robert Frost

Something there is that doesn't love a wall,
That sends the frozen-ground-swell under it,
And spills the upper boulders in the sun,
And makes gaps even two can pass abreast.
The work of hunters is another thing:
I have come after them and made repair
Where they have left not one stone on a stone,
But they would have the rabbit out of hiding,
To please the yelping dogs. The gaps I mean,
No one has seen them made or heard them made,
But at spring mending-time we find them there.
I let my neighbor know beyond the hill;
And on a day we meet to walk the line
And set the wall between us once again.
We keep the wall between us as we go.
To each the boulders that have fallen to each.
And some are loaves and some so nearly balls
We have to use a spell to make them balance:
'Stay where you are until our backs are turned!'
We wear our fingers rough with handling them.
Oh, just another kind of out-door game,
One on a side. It comes to little more:
There where it is we do not need the wall:
He is all pine and I am apple orchard.
My apple trees will never get across
And eat the cones under his pines, I tell him.

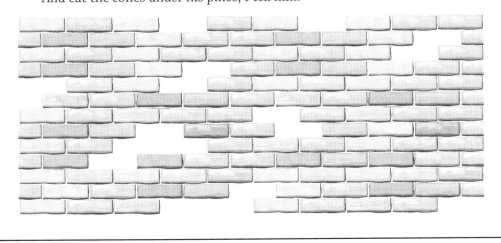

He only says, 'Good fences make good neighbors'.
Spring is the mischief in me, and I wonder
If I could put a notion in his head:
'Why do they make good neighbors? Isn't it
Where there are cows?
But here there are no cows.
Before I built a wall I'd ask to know
What I was walling in or walling out,
And to whom I was like to give offence.
Something there is that doesn't love a wall,
That wants it down.' I could say 'Elves' to him,
But it's not elves exactly, and I'd rather
He said it for himself. I see him there
Bringing a stone grasped firmly by the top
In each hand, like an old-stone savage armed.
He moves in darkness as it seems to me
Not of woods only and the shade of trees.
He will not go behind his father's saying,
And he likes having thought of it so well
He says again, "Good fences make good neighbors."

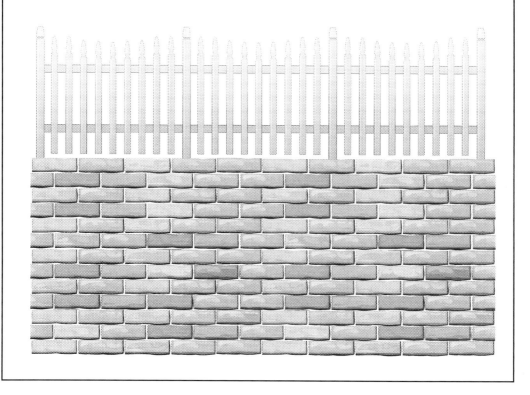

Name: _____

"Mending Wall"

Directions: Select one of the following options. ▲

Create a mind map of events that may lead to the wall needing to be mended.

Draw a picture that shows the scene depicted in this poem.

Free choice: Submit a free choice proposal about "Mending Wall" to your teacher for approval.

- -

"Mending Wall"

Directions: Select one of the following options. ●

Use a Venn diagram to compare the two neighbors in "Mending Wall."

Create a collage of ideas, sayings, or rules that help people be good neighbors.

Write a three facts and a fib about the characters of "Mending Wall."

- -

"Mending Wall"

Directions: Select one of the following options. ■

Do you agree with the last line in the poem? Record a documentary that discusses this adage and supports the opinion of the speaker or his neighbor.

Write a story that shares the reasons for the wall now and the original reasons behind its construction.

Create a scrapbook of at least five other poems that have a similar style to this one. Write a paragraph for each poem to defend its inclusion in the scrapbook.

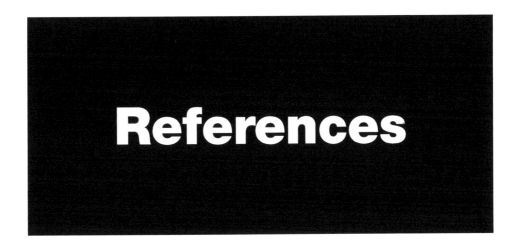

References

Anderson, L. W., & Krathwohl, D. R. (Eds.). (2001). *A taxonomy for learning, teaching, and assessing: A revision of Bloom's taxonomy of educational objectives.* New York, NY: Allyn & Bacon.

Cipani, E. (1995). Inclusive education: What do we know and what do we still have to learn? *Exceptional Children, 61,* 498–500.

Keen, D. (2001). *Talent in the new millennium: A two-year research study of gifted education.* Retrieved from http://files.eric.ed.gov/fulltext/EJ854972.pdf

About the Author

After teaching science for more than 15 years, both overseas and in the U.S., **Laurie E. Westphal** now works as an independent gifted education and science consultant nationwide. She enjoys developing and presenting staff development on differentiation for various districts and conferences, working with teachers to assist them in planning and developing lessons to meet the needs of all students. Laurie currently resides in Houston, TX, and has made it her goal to convert as many teachers as she can to the differentiated lifestyle in the classroom and share her vision for real-world, product-based lessons that help all students become critical thinkers and effective problem solvers.

If you are interested in having Laurie speak at your next staff development day or conference, please visit her website, http://www.giftedconsultant.com, for additional information.

Common Core State Standards Alignment

This book aligns with an extensive number of the Common Core State Standards for ELA-Literacy. Please visit http://www.prufrock.com/ccss to download a complete packet of the standards that align with each individual menu in this book.

Printed in the United States
by Baker & Taylor Publisher Services